Jimmy Butler: The Inspiring Story of One of Basketball's Best All-Around Shooting Guards

An Unauthorized Biography

By: Clayton Geoffreys

Table of Contents

Foreword

When Derrick Rose went down with the first major setback of his NBA career, the Chicago Bulls faced a predicament in which they were without their superstar for the next season. It was a heartbreaking tribulation for Bulls fans, but all hope was not lost. It did not take long before a new star arose from the Bulls' roster. That star was Jimmy Butler. In the light of Rose's string of injuries, Jimmy Butler came to establish himself as one of the key leaders of the Chicago Bulls franchise. His high degree of athleticism combined with his ability to be one of the few two-way players of the NBA has made him one of the new stars of the NBA. In the summer of 2017, Butler was traded from the Bulls to the Minnesota Timberwolves, marking the end of Butler's time with the Bulls. Butler's stint with the Timberwolves was short – he was traded to the Philadelphia 76ers in the 2018-2019 season, where he finished the season before signing with the Miami Heat in the 2019 offseason. It will be exciting to see what Jimmy is able to accomplish as a member of the Heat. Thank you for purchasing *Jimmy Butler: The Inspiring Story of One of Basketball's Best All-Around Shooting Guards*. In this unauthorized biography, we will learn Jimmy Butler's incredible life story and impact on the game of basketball. Hope you enjoy and if you do, please do not forget to leave a review!

Also, check out my website at claytongeoffreys.com to join my exclusive list where I let you know about my latest books. To thank you for your purchase, you can go to my site to download a free copy of *33 Life Lessons: Success Principles, Career Advice & Habits of Successful People*. In the book, you'll learn from some of the greatest thought leaders of different industries on what it takes to become successful and how to live a great life.

Cheers,

Clayton Geoffreys

Visit me at www.claytongeoffreys.com

Introduction

Finding the road to success usually comes with a few bumps along the way. Those can include having to deal with a period of not having a permanent home and trying to find places to stay on a nightly basis or having your family kick you out of your home and forcing you to rely on yourself. Sometimes, rewards await those who persevere, and Jimmy Butler is a perfect example of that.

Butler's case of starting from poverty to basketball stardom is not a rare one. There have been many players that have gone through similar circumstances. Allen Iverson and his family had lived in deep poverty before he broke out of it when he started starring in Georgetown in college. Kevin Durant was similarly situated. His mother had to support him and his brother by herself as they jumped from apartment to apartment. Even LeBron James had to suffer through poverty when his mom had him in her teens. However, Butler's story has a slight difference in how those other basketball superstars got out of poverty. Jimmy had to work his way up to it intensely.

The thing about Jimmy Butler is that his NBA stardom was not as apparent and as quick as some of the league's best players. His debut did not carry the same weight as some of his peers who came straight out of high school or after just one season in college basketball. Butler played his freshman year at a junior college and then three years at Marquette University where he finished his studies in communication studies. Even at Marquette, he was not a standout college player.

He rarely played when he first got to the big leagues, at least before others above him were injured. He was merely a project in his rookie year. He hardly played any games and could not even stay for more than ten minutes on the floor. When he got to his second year, an injury-laden Bulls team was forced to give him minutes. He was called upon merely for his ability to play defense. His offensive game was still a work in progress.

Every season, Jimmy Butler started showing signs of promise. The Chicago Bulls desperately needed offense as their sole scorer Derrick Rose was struggling to get back from injury. On a team built on players that specialized in defense, Jimmy Butler had to work his way to build an offensive repertoire good enough to be the Chicago Bulls' first option on offense. Eventually, he became their franchise star but has yet to become a serious MVP contender or even a superstar that could singlehandedly turn a team around.

Despite that, he continues to get better. Consider it the fruits of the labor of someone who did not want to fail. Maybe those fruits were planted by seeds from someone who wanted not to let his rough childhood define who he was; a young teenager who became homeless because his mom could not stand to look at him. Jimmy rose up from obscurity to become an elite two-way player in the league.

Fans know him as a workhorse of a player who is more than willing to play every second of the game – including overtime – just to help the team get another win. It does not matter if they are playing in the season-opener against the worst team in the league or a game against the defending NBA champions. In addition to his dedication, there is a reason he has been nicknamed "Jimmy Buckets."

In January 2016, he could set a career-high in points with 53, which made him the first in the Chicago Bulls franchise since Jamal Crawford in 2004 to have 50 or more points. A few weeks before that, he broke Michael Jordan's record for most points in a single half with 40 over the Philadelphia 76ers. "Jimmy gets buckets," as Chicago's broadcast crew said every time Butler went for a high-scoring game.

Those are just some of the highlights that have led Butler to make a name for himself in the league where he has surpassed the former top overall draft selection and other Chicago veterans to become an elite player that could play both ends of the floor. However, not even the way Butler has worked his way up to become a star made him an appreciated player in Chicago.

When the Chicago Bulls underwent a transition period from 2015 to 2017, Butler was still the main man of the team, but rumors of a trade started surfacing. Jimmy was still in the prime of his athletic form and was still getting better every season. However, he and the Bulls' top brass could not see eye-to-eye, and their relationship started dwindling as the franchise made questionable decisions and botched moves. While Butler wished to stay in Chicago, the Bulls had other plans. They traded him to the Minnesota Timberwolves during the 2017 offseason even after he posted career numbers across the board in his sixth season with the team.

Jimmy Butler was still an All-Star in Minnesota, and he led that team to its first postseason appearance since 2004. However, his stint with Minnesota did not last long because he did not see eye to eye with the other members of the team and the organization as well. Butler was eventually traded to the Philadelphia 76ers where he led the team to a second-round appearance in the playoffs. After that single season in Philly, he moved to the Miami Heat to become that team's best player.

Playing for a table organization like Miami will be very beneficial to Jimmy Butler, especially because of how competitive the Heat have always been. Above all, his ability to play defense at a high level fits in so well with the Heat's system. While he was not going to play with another All-Star in Miami unlike when he was with the Wolves and the 76ers, there is a solid reason to believe that he will be able to lead that team very well as their best player.

Chapter 1: Early Life & Childhood

Jimmy Butler was born on September 14, 1989, in a small suburb of Houston, Texas called Tomball. He did not have the greatest childhood as he was practically disowned by his family. When he was just a baby, his father left the picture, and he has yet to meet him. At age 13, his mother essentially told him that she did not like him at all and that he had to leave. This led to him being left with no other family to go to, nowhere to sleep, and no money on him – not the usual problems that a teenage boy has to deal with.

He did not speak much about it until 2011 when Butler interviewed with ESPN reporter Chad Ford about his childhood as he was preparing for the NBA Draft with workouts. It was a recollection of how he spent several years staying with friends for as long as possible. The stay usually lasted only a few weeks before he tried to find a new place to sleep at night. There was just one thing that kept Butler out of trouble when the teenager lost connection with his family, and that was basketball.

Playing basketball became his life, and he tried to make the varsity squad at Tomball High School. His name was growing in the district, and he was also able to earn invitations to elite summer leagues to continue to build on that status while still in high school. Having to continuously find a temporary home continued through his high school years until he met Jordan Leslie – who happened to be from Tomball, Texas as well. He had followed Butler's play with the high school and even in summer league competition.

At one time, he could move in with one of his friends from high school, Jermaine Thomas, whose dad worked long shifts on the road as a semi-truck driver. It was just one of the many temporary homes that Butler had, but one that he was able to go to multiple times. During the summer before Butler's senior year at Tomball High School, Leslie challenged Butler to a three-point shooting competition. Butler was a little surprised but was willing to accept the challenger, who was three years younger. He found that Leslie had skills as a basketball and football player. The two became friends quickly, and Butler was invited to the Leslie home to play video games and spend a night. The two had a lot in common. Leslie did not have his father around for a portion of his childhood either as his father died after being involved in a car accident.

Leslie's mother was a little worried at first, and not just because word was going around that Butler was considered "trouble." Financially, it is tough to run a home with four children from a previous marriage, but that is what Michelle Lambert did after her first husband passed away. Her new husband at the time was bringing a few children of his own into the fray, which made the home feature a total of seven children. With that many already living in the house, would there be room for someone like Butler? It would have been easy to say, "There's no room." However, that was not the type of mentality that Lambert and her spouse shared. Although there were discussions, it was not an immediate decision.

At first, Lambert's husband said yes to Butler spending the night – but only for a night or two at a time. While Jordan Leslie was initially the one to invite Butler, it became commonplace for each of the children in the home to say that it was his or her turn to have Butler over for the evening. This provided Butler more time to stay there, and it alternated between all seven before the cycle repeated. Eventually, the parents could only submit to the fact that young Jimmy Butler was becoming a part of the family. In the end, Lambert offered Butler a place to stay – permanently.

Now, this meant that Butler had to abide by house rules– rules that he did not have until the time before his mother kicked him out of the house. Butler was treated just like the other seven children living in the home. For example, there was a curfew, a daily chores list, and he also to attend all classes on time and earn good grades. The goal was to make Butler a role model for the younger children in the house. Butler was the senior in high school who was attracting plenty of attention for being one of Tomball High School's star athletes. His high school career was about to take off during his senior season and eventually moved towards college basketball. That is because Butler had one less thing to worry about, knew where he was going to be able to sleep, and knew that there was a spot at the dinner table every night with his newfound family.

When it came to high school basketball, his skills improved quickly after finding his new home with his friend Leslie and his parents. As a junior at Tomball High School, Butler made his debut on the varsity roster for the 2005-06 season and scored an average of about ten points per game. The team finished 17-15 in the Texas 5A Region II, District 16, but they were not able to advance to postseason play. As a senior during the 2006-07 high school basketball season, Butler averaged about 19.9 points and 8.7 rebounds per game. It was no surprise that he was considered the team's Most Valuable Player as voted by his peers and coaches. The team did okay with a 16-12 record. In the district playoffs, the Tomball Cougars defeated Spring High School on February 13, 2007, by a score of 58-43. It was a short-lived triumph as the Cougars then fell to Klein Collins,

68-57, on February 16, 2007, to be eliminated from the District II tournament.

Butler was still playing at a decent level with the Cougars, but it just was not enough to attract any NCAA Division I programs at the time. At Tomball High School, both the coaches and school principal did not have faith that he would succeed. That was a big reason why the coaches did not help Butler send videos to college basketball scouts, and that eventually led to Butler not receiving any offers to play Division I basketball. This made it hard for some youths to want to continue. Butler had no shortage of excuses to fail, such as being kicked out by his mom, not having a relationship with his father while growing up, the constant moving around from house to house, and not having much support at the high school. This is where that new family connection that had been made thanks to Jordan Leslie, his siblings, and Michelle Lambert had the most impact.

Therefore, he had to settle with going to Tyler Junior College. As he gained interest after a good freshman season at the junior college level, Lambert continued to be the motherly figure that Butler did not have for a good portion of his childhood, which ended up being good for Butler's basketball career and education. Ever since she and her husband had told Butler that they allowed him to stay with them permanently, they wanted to make sure that he was not just going to a college for his basketball career. They wanted him to have a completed degree to act as a "Plan B" in case basketball did not work out in the end.

Chapter 2: College Years

Freshman Year

After not receiving any offers to attend an NCAA Division I basketball program, Butler settled to attend Tyler Junior College in Tyler, Texas, a very short drive for him from his home in Tomball. The Tyler Junior College Apaches were part of the National Junior College Athletic Association's Region XIV.

It was a decent season for Butler and his team that finished 25-4 on the season and only lost in the Region XIV Tournament's quarterfinal round on March 8, 2008, during a 123-121 game in triple overtime. While the team did not advance to the NJCAA Division I National Championship Tournament, Butler played in all 29 games and averaged 18.1 points, 7.7 rebounds, and 3.1 assists while making about 54.8 percent of his field goals, which included 42.2 percent behind the three-point line. Butler received a spot on the All-Region XIV's first team while helping the Apaches reach a national ranking within the top ten and the region's North Zone Division title for the first time in more than 20 years.

The thing about playing very well at a small college is that some interest might be gained by NCAA Division I programs looking for more talent. Considering how well Butler played in high school and how he could gain some experience in the one season at Tyler Junior College, there were scouts watching games near the end of the season that led to letters of interest for a potential transfer. He was a two-star junior college recruit who was ranked number 127 in the Top 200 junior college players by 247Sports.com. Among the schools of interest were the Iowa State Cyclones of the Big 12 Conference and the Mississippi State Bulldogs of the Southeastern Conference.

In the end, he accepted an offer from Marquette University thanks to a visit in the months after the Apaches' season ended, and he was given an official scholarship offer from the Golden Eagles. By the time the summer semester rolled around, Butler was already enrolled for classes and had started training for his sophomore season with a team wanting to stand out in the very competitive Big East Conference.

His head coach at the time, Buzz Williams, said that it might not have been the only school on Butler's list of programs who had contacted the Apache star, but the coach brought in Butler based on the word of someone on Marquette's roster who had played with Butler at Tyler Junior College. There was not any mail sent by Williams to Butler, and there was not an official visit to the Marquette University campus in Milwaukee, Wisconsin.

Williams has shared the story about how Butler went to a nearby McDonald's restaurant to fax his signed National Letter of Intent to make his transfer to becoming a Golden Eagle official.

Sophomore Year

He was not a part of the starting five for the Golden Eagles in his first year at the Marquette University campus. However, he established himself as one of the best players coming off the bench to help Marquette have another excellent 20-plus win season. Granted, part of that could be credited to the fact that his coach was pretty strict, and he later admitted that the times he told Butler that he "sucked" as a running joke were a bit inhumane. However, the goal was to make him stronger and not quit. In the end, it worked, and Butler has not held a grudge from it since he has become a better player overall – starting with his years playing for the Marquette Golden Eagles.

In the season opener against Houston Baptist on November 14, 2008, Butler made all four free throws and a field goal to score six points during a 95-64 win. A few weeks later on December 2, 2008, Butler had seven points off the bench during their 81-67 win over Central Michigan, five of which were from the first half.

Butler continued to score points here and there, but there were times where he had some good rebound numbers in limited time. For example, he had five rebounds in less than 21 minutes on December 16, 2008, against Tennessee in an 80-67 loss. It was part of the Big East-Southeastern Conference Invitational event in Nashville, Tennessee. The very next night on December 19, 2008, Butler had seven points, six rebounds, and three assists in a 94-77 win over Western Carolina. A little more than a week later on December 28, 2008, Butler finished with eight points after making 75 percent from the field during Marquette's 84-45 win over Presbyterian College. It was the final game of Marquette's non-conference schedule where they started 11-2 before entering their Big East Conference schedule.

The Big East featured an enormous amount of talent that had grown enough that six of the teams finished ranked in the Top 25 after the season ended, and half of the conference had more than 20 wins in the season. As the Big East Conference schedule began, Butler scored more points as the lead reserve player for the Golden Eagles. On January 7, 2009, Butler had all nine of the points off the bench while also blocking a shot and getting a steal as they defeated Rutgers on the road, 81-76. Later in the month against Georgetown on January 31, 2009, Butler made all of his shots (two field goals and five free throws) to lead the Marquette reserves with nine points to help get a 94-82 win over the Hoyas.

In the game against South Florida on February 6, 2009, Butler had eight rebounds – which was a season-high for him at that point – despite the team losing 57-56 in Tampa, Florida. On February 17, 2009, he made four out of his six field-goal attempts to finish with eight points and seven rebounds during a 79-67 win over Seton Hall. The team lost six of the last nine games on the Big East Conference schedule, but Butler saw more minutes coming off of the bench and saw his average grow.

During a 93-82 loss to the Connecticut Huskies, also known as UConn, Butler made three of six field goals and all six shots from the foul line to finish with 12 points while collecting four rebounds, one block, and one steal on defense. On March 1, 2009, on the road against the Louisville Cardinals, Butler had ten rebounds for the first time in his early Marquette career to go along with converting on 40 percent from the field for six points. Later that week, Butler got his first collegiate double-double against the Syracuse Orange after scoring 14 points on four of nine from the field and four of six free throws to go along with 14 rebounds, four assists, and one steal.

After having a rough end to the regular season, Marquette got a first-round win during the Big East Conference Tournament over St. John's on March 11, 2009, with a 74-45 rout. Butler made all four field goals and all three free throws to have 11 points in addition to having nine rebounds and three assists. In the second round of the conference tournament on March 12, 2009, Butler led all players with 13 of 16 free throws and another three of five from the field to total 19 points. He also collected three rebounds, three steals, and blocked a shot, but the Golden Eagles lost to the Villanova Wildcats, 76-75.

After having a 24-9 record after the conference tournament, the Golden Eagles were still considered as a strong team to earn an at-large bid to be one of seven teams from the Big East to enter the NCAA National Championship Tournament. They were the sixth seed in the West Region of the bracket with their games starting in Glendale, Arizona. In the first round on March 20, 2009, Butler had just two points with four rebounds, two steals, and one assist during the team's 58-57 win over 11th-seed Utah State. The Golden Eagles then ran into the third-seeded Missouri Tigers on March 22, 2009, and lost 83-79 in a game where Butler made two of six from the field and three of four free throws to finish with seven points, three rebounds, one assist, and one steal.

At the end of the season, Butler played in all 35 games for the Golden Eagles and made 51.4 percent of his field goals, and averaged about 5.6 points, 3.9 rebounds, and just under one assist per game with his appearances coming off of the bench. In 22 of Marquette's games, Butler was the leading scorer coming off the bench, which included the team's final 15 games of the year during their appearance in the NCAA Tournament. This performance earned him Marquette's "Super Sub" award at the team's end of the season awards ceremony.

Junior Year

In the 2009-10 season with the Golden Eagles, Butler found himself joining the starting roster, which came with an increased number of minutes and offensive opportunities. During the season opener against Centenary College, he made 11 of 16 from the field and all five free throws to finish with 27 points and 13 rebounds during an 85-62 win on November 13, 2009. It was the first of a four-game home winning streak where the Golden Eagles were able to defeat teams like Maryland Eastern Shore, Grambling State, and South Dakota.

Marquette then traveled to Orlando, Florida for the Old Spice Classic tournament where the Golden Eagles won two out of three, starting with a 71-61 win over the Xavier Musketeers on

November 26, 2009. Butler scored 15 points after making four of five from the field and seven of ten free throws as a supporting player to Lazar Hayward's 27 points. Butler followed that performance up with 17 points and nine rebounds after making five of nine from the field and seven of eight on the foul line to help Marquette defeat the Michigan Wolverines, 79-65, on November 27, 2009. The Golden Eagles lost 57-56 to Florida State on November 29, 2009, with Butler scoring just ten points with 11 rebounds. Butler had a second consecutive double-double after having 19 points and 12 rebounds in the next game on December 5, 2009, in a 77-72 loss to North Carolina State.

Butler still had some impressive games despite having a few lower scoring outputs as he had against Florida State. On March 21, 2010, on the road in a conference game against the Cincinnati Bearcats, Butler tied with Darius Johnson-Odom for the most points for Marquette with 20 during a 79-76 overtime victory. Butler made five of nine from the field, including one three-point attempt, and another nine of ten from the free-throw line. He also had seven rebounds, three assists, two steals, and one blocked shot.

During his junior season with Marquette, Butler had a few game-winning shots to highlight his first season as a full-time starter. On January 30, 2010, Butler made six of 12 from the field and nine of 12 from the foul line to finish with 31 points and seven rebounds against the UConn Huskies. Butler made a baseline jumper with 2.4 seconds left in the game for the 70-68 win against the team that was ranked 19th nationally at the time. A few weeks later on February 24, 2010, at St. John's University in New York, Butler struggled from the field with four of 14 converted, but he still scored 18 points with eight rebounds and a block that featured another baseline jumper for the 63-61 win in overtime right before the buzzer sounded. It was during games like this where Butler was building the most confidence to be a strong player overall.

What's interesting is that Marquette went into overtime for a third consecutive game (all were wins) on February 28, 2010, while visiting Seton Hall. The Golden Eagles held on for an 84-83 overtime win as Butler made just three of seven from the field and seven of ten on the foul line for 13 points. He struggled in the first half with just five points to show at halftime.

After defeating the Louisville Cardinals in a game on March 2, 2010, where Butler had just eight points and five rebounds in the 69-48 win, Butler made some key baskets in yet another overtime thriller at home against the Notre Dame Fighting Irish on March 6, 2010. He went five of ten from the field and five of six free throws to finish with 16 points, eight rebounds, and four steals. The Golden Eagles could not win this overtime game. The Fighting Irish got the 63-60 win thanks to 18 points from Tim Abromaitis and a double-double by Carleton Scott (14 points, 13 rebounds) during the regular-season finale.

After some struggles in the Big East Conference schedule, Marquette wanted to advance beyond the first couple of rounds to earn an at-large berth in the NCAA National Championship Tournament. In the first round on March 10, 2010, Marquette was led by Lazar Hayward's 20 points in a 57-55 win. Butler scored just three points after one field goal and one free throw on 25 percent shooting. Butler had a much better game in a second-round upset of then eighth-ranked Villanova by a score of 80-76 on March 11, 2010. Butler made five of eight field goals and four of six free throws to finish with 14 points, eight rebounds, four assists, and two steals. The Golden Eagles dropped in their quarterfinals match with Georgetown, 80-57, on March 12, 2010, in a game where Marquette made just 37 percent of their field goals. Butler himself led the team with 17 points after making six of 12 field goals and four of five free throws while also collecting five rebounds.

With 22 wins on the season and while playing in one of the toughest conferences in the country, Marquette did receive an at-large bid – quality wins over ranked teams will help with that (i.e., defeating Villanova in the conference tournament). They were placed in the NCAA National Championship Tournament's East Regional as a sixth-seed to face the 11th seed Washington Huskies out of the Pacific-10 Conference who had a 24-9 record going into the tournament. In the first-round game on March 18, 2010, in San Jose, California, Washington's Quincy Pondexter drove past Butler for the layup that gave the Huskies the 80-78 win. Butler had a rough game, making just 33 percent from the field for eight points, four rebounds, and three steals.

While Washington advanced to the Sweet 16 round of the NCAA Tournament, the Golden Eagles wrapped up their season with a 22-12 record. Butler had a great breakout year for Marquette, making 53 percent from the field and 50 percent beyond the three-point line for season averages of 14.7 points, 6.4 rebounds, two assists, and a little more than one steal per game. Those numbers were good enough for Butler to earn an honorable mention on the All-Big East team for the 2009-10 season.

Senior Year

Butler returned for the Golden Eagles' 2010-11 season as the senior captain and made an immediate impact in the first few games of the season. It started with a 97-58 win on November 12, 2010, where Butler scored 18 points after making seven of 12 field goals and collected six rebounds, three assists, three blocks, and two steals. Later in the month on November 20, 2010, Butler scored 20 points and collected nine rebounds after making six of 11 field goals to help Marquette earn an 82-69 win to start the season 4-0.

The Golden Eagles suffered their first loss of the season on November 22, 2010, during the Hall of Fame Classic in a close match with the Duke Blue Devils, who were ranked first overall in the country, by a score of 82-77. Butler had a great game by scoring 22 points after making nine of 19 from the field and four of six from the foul line. He also collected six rebounds and had two steals on defense. Marquette lost their second consecutive game against another ranked team in the Gonzaga Bulldogs (number 22 at the time) on November 23, 2010, falling 66-63. Butler had another 22 points after making seven of 13 from the field including two of five behind the three-point arc. Butler also had six rebounds and made six of nine from the foul line to help the Golden Eagles in the loss.

After the losses, Butler had some struggles scoring in Marquette's wins over Wisconsin-Milwaukee (three of nine field goals for 13 points) and Longwood (two of seven from the field for eight points). He rebounded by making 71.4 percent from the field while scoring 15 points and collecting nine rebounds, three assists, and two steals on December 7, 2010, in an 86-50 win over Texas A&M Corpus Christi. Near the end of Marquette's non-conference schedule for the season, Butler had his first double-double during an 81-52 win at home over Centenary on December 18, 2010. Butler scored ten points after converting three of nine field goals and four of five free throws to go along with 12 rebounds. Butler followed that up on December 21, 2010, against Mississippi Valley State (102-77 win) where he had 17 points, four rebounds, three assists, and one steal. He then had 15 points, four rebounds, two assists, and one steal during a 77-76 loss on the road against the then-24th ranked Vanderbilt Commodores.

Having a 9-4 record before the conference schedule was not a bad thing, except the Big East Conference was a power conference in NCAA Division I basketball, as they usually are, with seven of the 16 teams ranked by the end of the season. It helped that they were able to get some wins to start the Big East schedule on January 1, 2011, during a 79-74 win, but Butler did not have to do much. Jae Crowder scored 29 points after making 12 of 14 field goals with Butler scoring ten points, seven rebounds, six assists, and a couple of blocks and steals. Butler had a better game against Rutgers on January 5, 2011, during a 73-65 win where he had 16 points, six rebounds, and a steal on defense.

Marquette dropped seven of their next 11 games with most of their losses coming against teams ranked in the nation's top 25. Butler had a few good individual performances despite the struggles the Golden Eagles were going through against the top-tier competition. For example, Butler had 21 points after making seven of 14 from the field and all seven free throws during a 76-68 loss to the Connecticut Huskies (then ranked fifth in the nation) on January 25, 2011, to go along with eight rebounds and three assists. He later had 19 points and eight rebounds after making six of ten from the field (including both of his attempts from three-point distance) to support Jae Crowder's 25 points in a close 76-70 loss at home against the ninth-ranked Syracuse Orange on January 29, 2011. During the end of the unfortunate stretch of losses, Butler's best game came from an 80-68 loss on February 16, 2011, where he had 23 points after making nine of 13 from the field to go along with seven rebounds and a couple of assists.

The Golden Eagles had a three-game stretch where Butler had some success, starting with 16 points after making seven of nine from the field and both free throws to help Marquette get a 73-64 win over Seton Hall on February 20, 2011. He followed that up with another 16 points and seven rebounds to help the Golden Eagles get a crucial overtime upset over the UConn Huskies on February 25, 2011. While Marquette lost their last two games of the regular season, Butler had two of his best games of the season as far as individual achievements. On March 3, 2011, Butler led the Golden Eagles with 30 points after making seven of 15 field goals and 15 of 17 free throws during a 67-60 loss at home to the Cincinnati Bearcats. This was followed up with an 85-72 loss at Seton Hall on March 6, 2011, where Butler had 20 points after making four of 11 field goals and 11 of 13 free throws.

Then came the difficult Big East Conference Tournament held at Madison Square Garden, which provided Marquette a final opportunity to make their case to earn a spot in the NCAA National Championship Tournament. On March 8, 2011, Marquette defeated the Providence Friars by a score of 87-66 in a game where Butler made five of eight from the field and eight of ten on the foul line to finish with 19 points, ten rebounds, and eight assists for a near triple-double. Butler scored just nine points after making two of five from the field during their upset of 20th ranked West Virginia, 67-61, on March 9, 2011. The Golden Eagles struggled in the Big East quarterfinals on March 10, 2011, during an 81-56 loss to the then-14th ranked Louisville Cardinals. Butler had 14 points, six rebounds, and a couple of steals and blocks in the losing effort.

Because of having some wins against ranked teams with a 9-9 record in the challenging Big East Conference, Marquette was still given an at-large berth in the NCAA National Championship Tournament. The Golden Eagles were provided an 11th seed in the tournament and placed in the East Regionals, which was held in Newark, New Jersey. In the official second round of the tournament on March 18, 2011, Marquette could get a crucial victory over the Xavier Mountaineers with a 66-55 win where Butler had made five of eight from the field and five of six free throws to finish with 15 points, five rebounds, and four assists. The Golden Eagles were then able to continue their success against their Big East Conference rivals from Syracuse with a 66-62 win. Butler had ten points and five rebounds in the upset of the three-seed.

However, Marquette's luck ran out in the East Region's semifinals on March 25, 2011, against second-seeded North Carolina in an 81-63 loss where Butler had 14 points after making six of 12 field goals while also collecting six rebounds and two assists. Despite some struggles during the regular season, the Golden Eagles finished with a 22-15 record overall and had advanced to the National Championship tournament's Sweet Sixteen round. Butler had a decent season with 15.7 points per game while making 49 percent from the field featuring 34.5 percent behind the three-point line. He also averaged 6.1 rebounds, 2.3 assists, and a little more than one steal per game in his senior season.

In addition to his career at Marquette, he also had the opportunity to stand out at multiple All-Star events. In April 2011 during the NCAA National Championship Tournament's Final Four weekend at Reliant Stadium in Houston, Texas, Butler was part of the East team, which also featured players like Austin Freeman of Georgetown. They were to face the West team of Tristan Thompson (North Texas), Kenneth Faried (Morehead State) and Kalin Lucas (Michigan State). While the East lost 113-108, Butler was five for 12 for 41.7 percent from the field and finished with 12 points, six rebounds, four assists, and two steals in just 20 minutes.

Butler was among the collegiate players invited to the 2011 Portsmouth Invitational Tournament held April 6-9, 2011 in Portsmouth, Virginia. The camp, which dates back to 1963, is a camp and tournament where teams of collegiate seniors play each other over the course of four days. Notable alumni of the tournament have included Scottie Pippen, John Stockton, and Avery Johnson. Butler was selected to play with the K&D Rounds Landscaping team that also included Frank Hassell from Old Dominion and Rick Jackson from Syracuse. In the three games that he played, Butler averaged 18.7 points, 4.7 rebounds, four assists, and nearly one blocked shot per game while shooting about 62.1 percent from the field, all of which earned Butler Honorable Mention honors for the All-Big East awards which were handed out at the end of the season.

Considering how well he was playing during the event commonly referred to as the PIT, combined with the pre-draft ESPN article by Chad Ford, there was more interest from NBA teams who were considering Butler. So many general managers in the NBA were excited to give a player a chance, especially one who had worked hard to turn a tough personal situation around and earned his way to Division I basketball and the opportunity to be considered a future professional basketball player. In the end, he was a first-round selection by the Chicago Bulls at number 30.

Chapter 3: NBA Career

Getting Drafted

Physically, there was a lot to like about Jimmy Butler coming into the NBA Draft. Standing more than 6'7" with his shoes on, he had good height for a wing player. At 220 pounds, he had a robust physique that was good enough for the big leagues and for him to get physical with veteran players at his position. As far as his athleticism went, Jimmy Butler also showed good quickness and an above-average leaping ability to contend with any other wings in the NBA. He had pretty good physical attributes for his position.

Regarding Butler's offense, he uses his strength and physique to finish baskets inside the paint and during transition opportunities. He does not fear contact and is aggressive whenever he gets the chance to go for a physical play at the basket. That was why he was attempting a good number of free throws a night in his last two years in Marquette.

Jimmy Butler's offense is also predicated on his confident shooting, especially when he is in the mid-range area. Most of his spot-up shots are from within that two-point area on the floor while he has also shown vast improvement in creating his pull-up shots from the perimeter during his senior year in college. Where Jimmy Butler excels the most on the offensive end is his use of his basketball IQ. He does not need to dominate the ball to be an effective player. Instead, he would rather pick his spots and catch defenses off guard by making use of backcourt cuts. As far as his offense went, he did not have any glaring weaknesses in the skills needed for a serviceable wing player in the NBA.

Using his high basketball IQ, Jimmy Butler has also shown a good sense for making the right passes and creating plays for his teammates. He was always a willing passer in college and was highly unselfish. Butler never made passes that were too difficult. Instead, he settled on making passes he knew were efficient and safe. His assist/turnover ratio at Marquette was pretty good considering that he would rather make the simple pass rather than the highlight-reel play.

Jimmy Butler also showed promise as a rebounder with his great feel for the game. He knows how to get good rebounding position on both ends of the floor. Butler fought for possessions and got many tip-ins for Marquette in his three seasons with the team. If he could get the tips, he tried as hard as he could to keep possessions alive and to make sure that his team had an extra crack at the basket.

Defensively, Jimmy Butler had a lot about which to be happy. He is defensively tough and works hard on that end of the floor. Butler got plenty of deflections with his good anticipation and long arms. He scraps for loose balls and works hard to get the defensive glass for his team. Add the fact that, with his physique, he can be a real asset to cover all three perimeter positions in the league.

However, the greatest crack at Jimmy Butler was that he never excelled at any particular area of the game. He had excellent skills all-around. He could finish, shoot, pass, rebound, and defend. However, none of those skills were remarkable enough for him to stand out. He was a "jack of all trades" that did not specialize in any skills.

Athleticism-wise, he does not wow anyone with his leaping abilities or his tendency to make highlight plays. While Butler is athletic enough for the NBA, many critics point out that he does not have the standout athleticism to make up for his lack of polished and elite skills at any facet of the game. He was even described as a player that did not have enough athletic ability to play one-on-one or keep up defensively with the best in the league.

When it comes to his shooting, Jimmy Butler may have shown improvement and steadiness at the mid-range. With the way the NBA has trended towards using wings to stretch the floor to the three-point area, Jimmy Butler needed plenty of work on his shooting range considering that he never showed enough consistency with his three-point shot.

Numerous critics also pointed out that Jimmy Butler did not have All-Star potential in him. The best that some said that he could reach is the level of a player like Wesley Matthews. Matthews was good enough to be a starter and a productive perimeter player but never got to the degree of a star despite his abilities to play both ends of the floor well. At best, Jimmy Butler was described as a coveted role player because of his excellent all-around skills, basketball IQ, and attitude. If he could improve his shot, some even said that he had a chance of being a standout rotation player from the bench.

If there was one thing that scouts overlooked about Jimmy Butler, it was that he was a workhorse. Butler's work ethic and determination to improve was always his best attribute. He spent hundreds of hours in the gym to develop his game. What he showed in his last two years in Marquette was a product of repetition inside the gym. He may not have had all the physical tools or potential to be great, but Butler showed the entire world that hard work beats talent when talent does not work hard.

When the draft day came, consensus top overall pick Kyrie Irving was chosen by the Cleveland Cavaliers with the first pick. It then took 28 more picks later for Jimmy Butler's name to get called. The Chicago Bulls, with the 30th overall draft pick, selected Jimmy Butler out of Marquette hoping he was a serviceable role player for them in the future, especially playing under a defensive team that dominated the league the previous season. However, as his journey was, Butler was eventually more than just a rotational player.

Rookie Year

Entering the National Basketball Association at six-foot-seven and 220 pounds, there was a lot to like physically about Butler. However, there were numerous fans in Chicago who were not happy about the selection because they felt that the Bulls needed to have more power in their offense to complement Derrick Rose. According to a former Chicago Bull and color commentator for Bulls radio broadcasts, Butler did not enter the NBA known for that sort of play, and he was more expected to be a fill-in from the bench who could make some defensive plays.

Butler's NBA debut was delayed, considering that there was a player lockout that had shortened the season. After a new collective bargaining agreement was made between players and owners, Butler was officially able to sign his first NBA contract with the Chicago Bulls on December 9, 2011. Instead of an 82-game regular season, the Bulls and all other 29 teams had to play a much more condensed 66-game season that made things tough for everyone.

The thing about the Chicago Bulls this season was that Butler was joining a very talented roster that featured Derrick Rose as the point guard and central point of the Bulls' offense, who averaged 21.8 points per game and made 43.5 percent from the field. The three-year young star was also joined by NBA veterans Luol Deng, Carlos Boozer, and Richard Hamilton, and they were why the reason why the Bulls was one of the top teams in the league with a 50-16 record in the shorter season. This built on top of the momentum of Tom Thibodeau's first season as head coach where they went 62-20 in the 2010-11 season.

Because of the star power that the Bulls had, Butler's opportunities in Chicago were few and far between. Having playing minutes here and there in 42 games, Butler's averages were low at about 2.6 points and 1.3 rebounds. Butler made his debut a few games into the season on January 1, 2012, where he played a little more than five minutes and scored his first field goal for two points and his first two rebounds during a 104-64 win over the Memphis Grizzlies. After playing less than a minute in Chicago's wins over the Atlanta Hawks and Detroit Pistons, Butler was very efficient in just 12 minutes in Atlanta, making all three field goals and all six free throws to finish with 12 points during the team's 109-94 loss to the Hawks on January 7, 2012.

There were not many more games where Butler scored into the double digits. He came close multiple times during a three-game stretch in the month of March. On March 10, 2012, during a home game against the Utah Jazz, Butler made two of four from the field and four of six from the foul line to finish with eight points and five rebounds as the Bulls defeated the Jazz 111-97. In the very next home game against the New York Knicks on March 12, 2012, Butler played nearly 29 minutes while making three of seven field goals and two out of three free throws to finish the game with eight points. He also collected two rebounds, one assist, and a steal with Chicago taking the 104-99 win. Butler followed that up with another eight points despite making just one of five field goals (he converted all six free throws) in just 12 minutes in Chicago's 106-102 win on March

14, 2012. The only other game where Butler scored in double figures was during the final game of the regular season in a 107-75 win over the Cleveland Cavaliers. Butler was a reserve that played 28 and a half minutes to convert on 50 percent of his field goals and just over than half of his free throws to score 12 points while collecting four rebounds and two assists. Many reservists had opportunities to perform since players like Rose were taking the night off to prepare for the upcoming playoffs.

Speaking of the playoffs, the Bulls easily won the Central Division with that 50-16 record, which tied them for the best record in the league with the San Antonio Spurs. Now the Bulls were the first overall seed in the Eastern Conference for the upcoming NBA playoffs. However, the Bulls made history they were not necessarily hoping for by losing in the first round of the playoffs to an eighth-seed team.

In the final moments of Chicago's 103-91 win in the first game of the best-of-seven series, Rose suffered a left knee injury after attempting to jump off of his left foot after having 23 points, nine assists, and nine rebounds, which prompted medical staff at the United Center to help him off of the court. The results of the subsequent tests showed that Rose had suffered a torn ACL in his left knee and that he was not going to play for the remainder of the NBA Playoffs. The Bulls were able to get one more victory before eventually losing the series in six games to be eliminated quicker than anyone else in the league expected. Butler made appearances in three of the games. In Game 3 on May 4, 2012, he played just three and a half minutes in the 79-74 loss. In the next game on May 6, 2012, during an 89-82 loss in Philadelphia, he played only 11 seconds near the end of the match. In the final game of the series on May 10, 2012, in a 79-78 loss, Butler's time increased only slightly with just 26 seconds. In all three of his appearances against the 76ers, Butler did not have the opportunity to make any field goals, free throws, rebounds, or assists.

The Bulls fell apart unexpectedly, and the team was hoping they could start making some roster improvements to help with the fact that Rose had a very long road to recovery from the ACL tear. There were some changes made and during the summer offseason, and Butler was one of the members of the Chicago Bulls' squad that played in the NBA Summer League for a short five-game stint.

Butler averaged 20.8 points, 6.5 rebounds, two assists, and almost one steal per game. One of his best games of the 2012 Summer League was during a 79-74 loss to the Boston Celtics on July 17, 2012. He led the game with 25 points after making seven of 16 field goals and another ten of 12 from the foul line while also collecting seven rebounds, three assists, and one steal.

In the very next game on July 18, 2012, in a 96-88 loss to the Houston Rockets, Butler scored another 24 points after making six out of 11 field goals (including his single attempt beyond the three-point line) and a near-perfect 11 of 12 free throws. Butler also collected another seven rebounds with one assist and one steal. With numbers like that, there was a chance that Butler was going to start earning more time for the 2012-13 NBA season, even though there were players like Luol Deng who got the starting role ahead of Butler.

Cracking the Rotation

Before the beginning of his second season in the NBA, the Chicago Bulls decided to exercise their third-year option on Butler's rookie contract on October 30, 2013. This meant that the Bulls already intended to extend his contract to the third year though Butler was only just about to participate in his sophomore season in the NBA.

Butler did not see much time right away, but he was making the most of his opportunities, such as making three of four from the field and both free throws to finish a 115-86 win over the Cleveland Cavaliers with eight points, four rebounds, and one assist on November 2, 2012. In the first 37 games of the season, Butler averaged about five points and nearly three rebounds per game while making 49.3 percent from the field. That span also showed him scoring in the double digits twice with 13 points during a 101-78 win over the Dallas Mavericks on November 28, 2012, and in a 97-81 loss to the Phoenix Suns on January 12, 2013.

While the minutes were limited for the first half of the season, Butler had a more significant role when Luol Deng suffered an injury of his own against the Memphis Grizzlies on January 19, 2013. Butler got his first career start on January 21, 2013, and played a little more than 43 minutes to make just four of ten field goals and both free throws to score ten points, eight rebounds, four assists, and one steal in a 95-83 win over the Los Angeles Lakers.

Butler followed that up in the very next game on January 23, 2013, during an 85-82 win over the Detroit Pistons. He had 18 points after making six of 14 from the field (one out of four behind the three-point line) and a nearly perfect five of six free throws while also collecting nine rebounds, four assists, one steal, and one blocked shot. In the very next game on January 25, 2013, against the Golden State Warriors, Butler had his first career double-double with 16 points after shooting 60 percent from the field and all four free throws while also collecting 12 total rebounds (eight of which were on defense), two assists, and one block.

That career-high in points fell on January 28, 2013, during a 93-85 win over the Charlotte Bobcats where Butler made seven of ten field goals and five of seven free throws to end the night with 19 points, six rebounds, two assists, and one block. The latter half of January gave Butler a very successful run where he averaged nearly ten points per game and almost five rebounds while making 50.5 percent of his field goals and another 33.3 percent behind the three-point line.

The month of February had a great start as well. Butler got his second career double-double after making six of 16 field goals and all three free throws to score 16 points while having ten rebounds, three steals, and two assists during a dominant 93-76 win on the road in Atlanta, Georgia on February 2, 2013.

When Deng returned to the Bulls, Butler was sent back to the bench. However, he was going to see more time on the court after the coaching staff saw how good he was playing on the court. Later in the season, Butler continued to improve as an offensive weapon. On March 3, 2013, while visiting the Indiana Pacers, Butler hit the 20-point mark for the first time after he made six out of 11 field goals that featured making three of five attempts behind the three-point line. He also collected four rebounds, two steals, and one assist in the 97-92 loss to the Pacers. Butler hit the 20-point benchmark a couple more times and found a new career-high in a few other games. That included another 20 points after shooting 45.5 percent from the field, hitting both of his shots from three-point range and eight of nine free throws to help the Bulls top the Minnesota Timberwolves, 104-97, on March 24, 2013. Additionally, it was a game where he collected nine rebounds, three steals, and two assists.

While Chicago lost to the Toronto Raptors, 101-98, on April 9, 2013, Butler had a new career-high mark with near-perfect efficiency. He made ten of 12 field goals (all three of his three-point shots were converted) and five of six free throws to have 28 points, seven rebounds, two steals, and two assists in a game where Butler played all 48 minutes of the regulation time. During the next game on the schedule, Butler played another 50 minutes in a 118-111 overtime thriller over the New York Knicks on April 11, 2013. Butler made nine of 15 from the field (two of three behind the three-point line) to finish with 22 points while having another 14 rebounds, three steals, three blocks, and two assists.

After having a record among the best in the league for the past two seasons, the Bulls were struggling with lack of depth and multiple players dealing with injuries. The team finished with a record of 45-37 and earned themselves the fifth seed in the Eastern Conference. It did not help when the news started to come out about how Derrick Rose was returning to practice earlier in January of that season with full contact. A few months later in March, he was cleared to play for the Bulls. That fact was mixed with many videos surfacing online of Rose performing slam dunks off of both his left and right foot. However, he was not pressured into rushing back onto the court by the team, and he did not feel as if he needed to play in the final months of the 2012-13 season, nor did he make an appearance in that playoff run for Chicago.

Despite going through a season without their number-one draft pick from the 2008 NBA Draft, Butler was becoming a strong young player for the franchise and was also becoming an integral part of Chicago's rotation after averaging nearly 41 minutes per game in the 2013 NBA Playoffs. Not bad for a second-year player that did not have the type of hype that came with players like Rose, LeBron James, or Kobe Bryant.

While his offensive numbers were improving, Butler was also getting a significant amount of numbers on the defensive side of the court. During the Bulls' 95-94 win over the Detroit Pistons on March 31, 2013, Butler had a season-high five steals in the game as a starter, which went along nicely with his 16 points and 57.1 percent field goal efficiency. The latter half of the season also featured Butler having two games with three blocked shots – March 18, 2013, versus the Denver Nuggets (119-118 loss), and April 11, 2013, versus the New York Knicks (118-111 win). After playing in all 82 games for the Bulls, Butler finished with an average of 8.6 points – six more than his rookie average – four rebounds, and about one assist and steal per game while making 46.7 percent from the field. Butler also improved his three-point accuracy from 18.2 percent in his rookie season up nearly 20 percent to 38.1 percent in his sophomore season in Chicago.

The Bulls found themselves facing the Brooklyn Nets (49-33) in the first round of the playoffs. Butler did more than just appear in the playoffs as he did during his rookie season where he had no attempted field goals. During Game 1 of the series against the Nets on April 20, 2013, Butler played nearly 40 minutes while making five of eight from the field and all three free throws to finish with 13 points, but the Bulls lost 106-89 in Brooklyn. In Game 2 on April 22, 2013, Butler only had five points in almost 30 minutes, but the Chicago defense could hold

Brooklyn to just 35.4 percent shooting from the field in a 90-85 win.

In Game 3 on April 25, 2013, Chicago had nearly half of its offense come from Boozer's 22 points and Deng's 21 points in a 79-76 win at home in Chicago to jump ahead in the series – Butler had just four points after shooting 20 percent from the field. With the defensive battles in the first three contests, both teams exploded offensively in Game 4 on April 27, 2013, where the Bulls defeated the Nets 142-134 in a triple-overtime game. While Nate Robinson came off the bench and led Chicago with 34 points and made 60.9 percent of his field goals, a total of seven Bulls scored in double figures. Butler made six of eight from the field and three of five on the foul line to finish with 16 points. He also collected five rebounds, three assists, and had one block and one steal.

The triple-overtime win gave Chicago the 3-1 series lead, and it looked like they were going to advance early. The Nets did not let up, and Chicago had some real issues with their overall depth because of injuries and with Rose not rushing back to the Bulls' lineup. Brooklyn took Game 5 on April 29, 2013, by a score of 110-91. Butler made five of nine field goals and five of eight free throws to have 18 points and four steals. The Nets then tied the series and forced a Game 7 after defeating Chicago 95-92 on

May 2, 2013. Despite struggling from the field with 30.8 percent shooting, Butler still finished the game with 17 points, seven rebounds, six assists, and another steal. While Butler had just nine points after playing all 48 minutes of Game 7 on May 4, 2013, the heroes for Chicago were Joakim Noah and Marco Belinelli, who each scored 24 points to help Chicago advance with a 99-93 win.

Chicago then found themselves against the top-seeded Miami Heat and were able to get the first game victory, 93-86, on May 6, 2013. Butler once again played all 48 minutes and finished with 21 points, 14 rebounds, and three assists to support Robinson's 27 points and nine assists. With less than ten active players on the team's roster, the Heat caught on fire in Game 2 with a 115-78 win on May 8, 2013, where Butler had a meager nine points, and the team had merely 35.5 percent shooting from the field. It was a little better in Game 3 in a 104-94 loss on May 10, 2013, at the United Center – Butler had 17 points, five rebounds, three assists, and three steals in another 48-minute marathon. The Bulls then had their worst playoff game in an 88-65 defeat at home on May 13, 2013. Butler made just 40 percent of his shots for 12 points while Boozer led Chicago with 14 points, and the team made just 25.7 percent of their overall field-goal attempts.

Miami closed out the series in Florida during Game 5 on May 15, 2013, in a 94-91 victory. Butler played much better with 19 points after making seven of 15 field goals and had five rebounds, four assists, and three steals. The Heat were the better team and had a lot more depth to their roster. This led the Heat, who were 66-16 in the regular season, to the NBA Finals to defeat the San Antonio Spurs in a thrilling seven-game series during the NBA Finals.

The Start of His Rise

Just a few days before the start of the regular season, the Bulls gave Butler another extension by going with the fourth-year option on his rookie contract so that he played through the 2014-15 NBA season. The Bulls had plenty of hope with the return of Derrick Rose after a few preseason tune-up games where he later told the media that he felt he could have a lot more potential to be explosive and that he could jump better with a supposed vertical jump increase of about five inches. During the preseason, Rose averaged nearly 21 points and about five assists per game.

In the first game of the season on October 29, 2013, Rose only had 12 points and four assists in about 34 minutes in a 107-95 loss to the Miami Heat. Rose averaged about 28.8 percent from the field during his return season with Chicago. As far as Butler was concerned, he had a much better game making six of 12 field goals including two of four from three-point range while making another six of seven free throws to finish with 20 points, five steals, three assists, three rebounds, and one steal. This was a much different performance than the one from the team's captain Rose, who struggled after having been gone for a little more than a year.

However, Butler had his own struggles early on in the season. During the team's home opener on October 31, 2013, against the New York Knicks, Butler made just 27.3 percent shooting from the field to score 11 points and ten rebounds for the double-double in the 82-81 win. He also had another three steals while playing imposing defense. The points were hard to come by during a three-game stretch where the Bulls lost two of those games. The one win on November 8, 2013, against the Utah Jazz (97-73) was Butler's worst offensive performance of the year with just five points, and he only made two of five field goals while also collecting four rebounds, three assists, and two steals.

The Bulls were starting to turn things around as they won five in a row that featured Butler averaging 10.8 points per game. On November 15, 2013, Butler scored 14 points after making all six free throws and three of seven from the field (two of those behind the three-point line) while also collecting seven rebounds, two assists, one steal, and one block. A few nights later on November 18, 2013, Butler had made another four of six from the field (both attempts from three-point range) and four of five free throws to have 14 points during an 86-81 win over the Charlotte Bobcats. He also had five rebounds and two steals. However, after playing 22 minutes, Butler injured a toe and found himself dealing with a nagging injury that cost him 11 games.

During the second game of that span on November 22, 2013, Rose suffered another knee injury against the Portland Trail Blazers. An MRI exam revealed that he had torn the meniscus in his knee. The required surgery was done a few days later, and the team announced that he would not return for the rest of the 2013-14 season. The good news for Rose was that the surgery was considered successful, but it left Chicago without their number-one overall draft pick from 2008. It was bad news for the Bulls as they were without their star player once again, and their rising star. So, for the 11 games without Butler, the Bulls only had two wins, and the once-dominant Chicago Bulls were falling below the .500 mark.

Butler returned to the Chicago lineup in Milwaukee, Wisconsin on December 13, 2013, and played a little more than 36 minutes in the starting lineup in a 91-90 win. He made four of 12 from the field while scoring 16 points and collecting three steals, two rebounds, and one assist. He had a little more accuracy in fewer minutes the next night at home on December 14, 2013, in a 99-77 loss to the Toronto Raptors. Butler made 66.7 percent from the field overall and behind the three-point line for 11 points, four rebounds, one steal, and one block. He started to hit his stride again on December 18, 2013, where he made 53.3 percent from the field to lead the Bulls with 20 points despite falling to the Houston Rockets, 109-94. Before the end of the month, Butler had one of the best games of his career on December 30, 2013. He made six of ten from the field and 12 of 14 free throws for a final line of 26 points, four rebounds, and two assists to help the Bulls defeat the Memphis Grizzlies, 95-91.

Butler had several games the previous season where he was willing to play every second of regulation. During a thrilling triple overtime game on January 15, 2014, where the Bulls were able to defeat the Orlando Magic, Butler played just over 60 minutes in the contest. Butler also had a pretty good game against Orlando, scoring 21 points and collecting seven rebounds, six assists, two steals, and two blocks despite shooting just 35.3 percent from the field.

Shortly after that game, his numbers started to improve again, and he grabbed a few more double-doubles before the end of the regular season during a second-half playoff push. On January 20, 2014, the Bulls reached the even .500 mark with a 102-100 win over the Los Angeles Lakers where Butler finished with 13 points, 11 rebounds, five assists, four steals, and one block. He also had 12 points and 13 rebounds and was selective in his shots (55.6 percent from the field) to help the Bulls earn the 100-85 win over the Atlanta Hawks on February 11, 2014.

One of his better games was later in that season, playing all but two minutes of a 105-94 win while visiting the Detroit Pistons on March 5, 2014. It was a game where Butler made seven of 15 from the field (46.7 percent) and a statistical line of 18 points, 12 rebounds, four assists, and three blocks. Later in the season as they were continuing to fight for a playoff berth, they were able to get a few upsets against teams like the Miami Heat on March 9, 2014, where Butler had another double-double with 16 points and 11 rebounds during a 95-88 win. While that game saw him struggle from the field, shooting only 26.7 percent, he played well on defense with another four steals and two blocked shots.

In the end, Chicago finished with a record of 48-34, enough to place second in the Central Division, with the Indiana Pacers having a breakout season with a 56-26 record. In 67 appearances for the Bulls, Butler logged an average of nearly 39 minutes, and his points per game improved to 13.1. He also averaged nearly five rebounds and almost two steals per game. This led to him being named to the second team of the NBA's All-Defensive team (other names included the Heat's LeBron James and the Pacers' Roy Hibbert). His teammate Joakim Noah was on the first team because of his ability to collect several rebounds and blocks on the defensive side of the court. His field-goal percentage dropped to just under 40 percent as he had a period of trying to find his scoring groove after the toe injury back in November 2013.

During Chicago's postseason in 2014, they were tied record-wise with the Toronto Raptors but did not have the tiebreaker as they were the fourth seed going into the Eastern Conference Playoffs. It was a grueling series where all games were within single-digits. The Washington Wizards took the first game in Chicago, Illinois, on April 20, 2014, with a 102-93 decision. Butler had 15 points after shooting 50 percent from the field, and he had had more points if he was better from the foul line (three of seven). Butler also had another seven rebounds, three steals, and two assists as the Bulls were led by 16 points from both Kirk Hinrich and D.J. Augustin.

The second game of the series on April 22, 2014, was even closer. The Wizards were the winners after holding a late rally in overtime with a final score of 101-99 in one of Butler's worst playoff games with only two of nine made field goals (missing all three-point attempts) to have six points, seven rebounds, two assists, and one steal. Chicago avoided being down 3-0 in the first-round series after taking Game 3 on April 25, 2014, by a score of 100-97. Butler still had 15 points despite making just three of seven from the field and seven of eight free throws. He also collected five rebounds, two assists, and a steal.

However, the Wizards were able to take Game 4 via a score of 98-89 on April 27, 2014, after Washington's Trevor Ariza led the team with 30 points with an efficient ten of 17 from the field. On Chicago's side, Taj Gibson was the leading offensive threat with 32 points after making 13 of 16 from the field (81.3 percent) and another six of seven on the foul line. Butler was the second-leading scorer for the Bulls with just 16 points after making five of 14 total field goals (35.7 percent). He struggled on the three-point line merely just two of seven beyond the arc.

Chicago's season ended during Game 5 on April 29, 2014, in a game where the Bulls made 33.3 percent from the field as a team, and the Wizards did slightly better, shooting 40.5 percent. Butler's 16 points were the best for Chicago as he made six of 15 field goals (40 percent) and two of four in three-point range. He also collected four rebounds, two assists, and one steal. Noah had success with 18 rebounds (16 on defense), seven assists, three blocks, and two steals, although he only had six points offensively.

Chicago's postseason run ended similarly to the year before when they had only so many players beyond the starting five. The loss during the fifth game of their first-round series with Washington was a perfect example of that as they had had only Taj Gibson, D.J. Augustin, and Tony Snell available on the bench with five players finding themselves unable to suit up for the game. That does not count the often-injured Derrick Rose.

The Wizards' success stopped in six games against the Indiana Pacers in the Eastern Conference semifinals, who in turn lost to the Miami Heat in the conference finals in another six games. This was another season where the NBA championship crown once again went to a familiar team from San Antonio – a team that had the right combination of veteran leadership and depth that made teams like the Spurs and Heat at the time the top contenders. With the injuries to key players, Chicago did not have that outside of Butler and a few other contributors. Therefore, the Bulls were about to make some significant changes to improve the Chicago lineup.

Becoming an All-Star

Before the season started, head coach Tom Thibodeau needed to make some roster adjustments before his fifth season leading the Bulls. That meant releasing veteran Carlos Boozer for another veteran big man, Pau Gasol, for a three-year contract worth about $22 million. Chicago also signed Nikola Mirotić from the Real Madrid Baloncesto club in Spain, as well as Aaron Brooks. Players who were able to be re-signed included reservists E'Twaun Moore and Nazr Mohammed.

However, the core focus was the hopefully healthier Rose, the newly-acquired Gasol, and the developing and rising star, Jimmy Butler. With all of the roster moves made and contracts signed, Chicago offered Butler a contract extension for about four years and worth about $44 million. For someone who was playing for just $2 million on his rookie contract and after having gone through so much adversity in his teenage years to get to this point, it was extremely tempting to find a pen and sign on the dotted line.

However, Butler decided to roll the dice, as some said, and play out the contract in the hopes that he had more significant offers as a restricted free agent before the 2015-16 season. Was it a risk? Yes. Was it worth it? It turned out to be because the 2014-15 season proved to be Butler's best season up to that point.

After missing the first two games of the season, Butler led Chicago with 24 points after making six of 12 from the field (50 percent) and a very efficient 11 of 15 from the foul line. This included the two free throws after he was fouled by Andrew Wiggins with the time expired in a 106-105 win on the road against the Minnesota Timberwolves on November 1, 2014.

In the very next game on November 4, 2014, at home against the Orlando Magic, Butler led the team again with seven of 15 field goals made (46.7 percent) and seven of 11 free throws (63.6 percent). He finished with 21 points, nine rebounds, three assists, two blocks, and one steal. Less than two weeks later on November 15, 2014, during a 99-90 loss to the Indiana Pacers, Butler had 32 points after making ten of 17 field goals (58.8 percent) and 11 of 14 free throws. He also had six rebounds, two steals, and one block on defense. It was to not be the only time Butler had a 30 points or more in a Chicago loss. On November 25, 2014, Butler made seven of 13 field goals and drew enough fouls to be able to boast making 18 of 20 free throws for a total of 32 points, a performance that almost featured a double-double with nine rebounds. This was also a game where the second-leading scorer was Gasol with 22 points, and many of the players had significantly underachieved, like Rose with only two points while playing less than ten minutes.

With an average of 21.9 points (which ranked in the top ten in scoring for the league), 5.7 rebounds, 3.1 assists, and 1.5 steals per game for 15 appearances in November, Butler was named the NBA Eastern Conference Player of the Month. It was an impressive period where Butler was playing nearly 40 minutes per game and still maintaining a respectable 49.8 percent field-goal percentage. It was not the end of the rise of Butler's popularity, either. Even the more casual basketball fanbase was starting to recognize the Chicago player wearing No. 21 and viewing him as superior above the one who wore jersey No. 1 (Rose).

Chicago was gradually becoming Butler's team, and he was becoming a more consistent offensive weapon than the former top overall draft selection. December provided many examples that proved that statement as fact, including Butler's performance in a 103-97 win over the New York Knicks on December 18, 2014. He made 11 of 21 field goals and nine of ten free throws to lead the game with 35 points, seven assists, five rebounds, four steals, and a blocked shot for good measure. In the very next game two nights later, Butler scored another 31 points in his first double-double of the season with ten rebounds while making another 11 of 21 field goals and all nine shots from the charity stripe. Joakim Noah had 13 rebounds of his own and Gasol had another 11 rebounds to show some of the potential the Bulls had moving forward.

In addition to having some big offensive numbers posted in his fourth season in the NBA, Butler was also providing plenty of defense to help Chicago. During a 129-120 win over the Toronto Raptors on December 22, 2014, Butler blocked five shots while also scoring 27 points and collecting 11 rebounds as Rose led the team with 29 points in one of his best games of the season. Later in the New Year on January 16, 2015, he collected a season-high of six steals in a game where he made 52.6 percent from the field for 22 points, five rebounds, and two more assists in a 119-103 victory over the Boston Celtics. Fast forward to February 8, 2015, in Orlando, Florida. Butler tied that season-high with another six steals in the 98-97 win over the Magic. While he led the team with 27 points after making 56.3 percent of his shots, one of Butler's five assists helped Rose hit a critical three-point field goal before Gasol hit the go-ahead layup with just nine seconds left.

While Butler's fame was slowly rising, he was still able to earn a spot in his first NBA All-Star Game as a reservist for the Eastern Conference on February 15, 2015, at Madison Square Garden in New York City. While the starters featured his Chicago teammate Gasol, Cleveland's LeBron James and Washington's John Wall, there was still plenty of talent on the bench for the East with Dwayne Wade making his 11th All-Star appearance and Chris Bosh making his 10th. While Butler only played for about nine minutes and 13 seconds, he was still able to score six points after converting on three of four field goals while also getting a couple of steals. However, the West won by a dizzying score of 163-158 in front of nearly 18,000 basketball fans.

Butler did not return to the Bulls' regular-season from the All-Star break with any form of rust. He made 50 percent of his field goals, featuring three of five from three-point range, while having a final statistic line of 30 points, five assists, and five rebounds that were the bright spot in a 100-91 loss to the Detroit Pistons on February 20, 2014. About a week later on February 28, 2015, Butler had another double-double with 28 points and 12 rebounds during a 96-89 game after making 11 of 19 of his field-goal attempts for 57.9 percent.

Unfortunately, Butler was ruled out due to an elbow injury he suffered during the March 1, 2015, loss to the Los Angeles Clippers (96-86) after having ten points on 33.3 percent shooting in less than 22 minutes. The injury's timetable for recovery usually falls within a three to six-week period, and the Butler-less Bulls went 5-6 during that 11-game stretch. The good news was that Butler returned to the team almost precisely on the three-week mark on March 23, 2015, in a 98-86 win over the Charlotte Hornets, and while he had 19 points and nine rebounds in the win, he struggled with shooting merely 30 percent from the field. That was quickly turned around by having near-perfect shooting after making seven of eight field goals and seven of nine free throws (he was also two of three behind the three-point arc) to finish with 23 points in the 116-103 win on the road in Toronto on March 25, 2015.

Chicago had a much better season than the one prior and finished with a record of 50-32, even though they were the runners-up in the Central Division again, this time behind the Cleveland Cavaliers (53-29). Even though the Bulls were not a division winner, they had a better record than the Atlantic Division's Toronto Raptors by one game (49-33) to earn the third seed for the Eastern Conference playoffs. During the season, Butler's offensive production continued to grow to per-game averages of 20 points, 5.8 rebounds, 3.3 assists, 1.8 steals, and just under one block per game, all while averaging a team-leading 38.7 minutes per game. Unlike the previous season, Butler's field-goal percentage rose nearly seven percent from 39.7 to 46.2 shooting from the field. He also improved his accuracy from three-point distance from 28.3 percent in the 2013-14 season to 37.8 percent in the 2014-15 season.

Because the Bulls were the third seed in the Eastern Conference, they were pitted against their fellow Central Division foes from Milwaukee. The Bucks were an even 41-41 with first-year head coach Jason Kidd and a very young corps of players that included Jabari Parker, O.J. Mayo, and the large Greek forward Giannis Antetokounmpo. This was a rare case of the Bulls having a fully healthy roster with Rose, Butler, Noah, and Gasol ready to enter the playoffs – which had the potential to do some damage in the Eastern Conference.

That combination made their presence known in the first game of the first-round playoff series with a 103-91 win on April 18, 2015. Butler led all Chicago players with 26 points after making eight of his 14 field goals (two of five three-point attempts) and seven of eight free throws. Rose followed that up with 23 points of his own while Gasol had 13 rebounds and Noah collected another 11 boards. Butler once again led Chicago in Game 2 on

April 20, 2015, with 31 points, nine rebounds, two assists, and one block in a 91-82 win over the Bucks. It was during this game that he shot 52.6 percent from the field, which included making three of nine from long distance. The Bulls then went up to a 3-0 lead in the series on April 23, 2015, led by Rose's 35 points and eight assists with 52.2 percent from the field (including five of nine from deep range) to give Chicago the 113-106 win. Butler had a decent game with 24 points after making 40 percent from the field while also playing excellent defense with three steals and two blocked shots.

While Chicago looked dominant in the first-round series, Milwaukee did not go away quietly and took the next two games in the series, starting with the Game 4 win to avoid the sweep on April 25, 2015, with a 92-90 win. That loss was due to a lack of offense outside of Butler scoring 33 points after making 70.6 percent from the field and12 of 17 field goals, which included five of seven from the three-point line, to go along with seven rebounds and another three steals. The Bucks kept their playoff hopes alive with a 94-88 win at the United Center in Chicago, Illinois after 22 points from Michael Carter-Williams and 21 points from Khris Middleton. Butler was one of three Bulls who had a double-double in the loss with 20 points, ten rebounds, and another six assists, four steals, and one block. The other two were Gasol (25 points, ten rebounds) and Noah (13 rebounds, ten points).

While the Bucks built up a little momentum, Chicago put the gas on and win Game 6 on April 30, 2015, by an astounding margin of 54 points with the final score at 120-66 for the Bulls' win. Butler had 16 points, five assists, and four steals while making seven of his 14 field goals (two of five from three-point range), but the unlikely scoring leader was Mike Dunleavy Jr. with 20 points, followed by 19 points and eight rebounds from Gasol.

This provided an exciting matchup for the Bulls as they were then up against the heavily-favored Cleveland Cavaliers who were a potent combination of players that featured LeBron James, the young Kyrie Irving, and veterans like Tristan Thompson and Mike Miller. With an injury that kept Kevin Love out of action, Chicago could take Game 1 in Cleveland, Ohio by a score of 99-92 on May 4, 2015. Butler made 43.8 percent from the field to finish with 20 points, six assists, five rebounds, and three steals. Rose was the leading scorer for Chicago with 25 points while Gasol was close behind with 21 points and ten rebounds.

Cleveland returned the favor as James scored 33 points and Irving had another 21 points in the Cavaliers' 106-91 win on May 6, 2015. Butler led Chicago with 18 points despite struggling, only making five out of 14 field-goal attempts (35.7 percent). Game 3 was a thriller with Butler making a two-foot jumper for a one-point lead while Rose hit a 26-foot three-point shot as time expired for the 99-96 win on May 8, 2015. Rose led Chicago with 30 points with seven rebounds and seven assists while Butler had 20 points, eight rebounds, and five steals on defense to contribute, giving the Bulls a 2-1 series lead in the Eastern Conference semifinals, which was the last highlight win for the Bulls that postseason.

On May 10, 2015, in Game 4, Cleveland had five players score in double figures, led by James' 25 points which were capped with a 21-foot baseline jumper for a buzzer-beating winner for the final score of 86-84. Rose's 31 points and Butler's 19 were the only double-digit efforts for a Chicago lineup that made just 36 percent from the field as a team. Butler and the Bulls had a better game overall during Game 5 on May 12, 2015, after he made 50 percent from the field, three of eight from three-point range, and all eight free throws to lead Chicago with 29 points, nine rebounds, and three assists. Cleveland was just a little bit stronger thanks to 38 points and 12 rebounds from James and another 25 points by way of Irving's hands in the 106-101 decision to give the Cavaliers a 3-2 lead going into the semifinal round.

With hopes of having some home-court magic on May 14, 2015, at the United Center, the Bulls struggled again as a team with a field-goal percentage of 37.5 during a 94-73 win for Cleveland to advance them to the Eastern Conference Finals. Butler was the bright spot for Chicago after he made eight of 22 field goals and both free throws to have 20 points and five rebounds. Rose was the only other double-digit offensive contributor with 14 points.

While Chicago was stronger, the Cavaliers proved to be the better team, and they moved on to a four-game sweep of the Atlanta Hawks in the Eastern Conference Finals before they lost in six games to the red-hot Golden State Warriors in the NBA Finals. Chicago was improving, but the amount of experience was still growing for still-young leaders like Butler and Gasol, who was starting to find his groove as a second big man alongside Chicago's veteran Noah. At least Bulls fans could say that James was denied another championship ring and was still behind the goal of Jordan's six rings for which James had been aiming.

The New Franchise Player

With an expiring contract, Butler had played worth a top-dollar value, and the Chicago Bulls were ready to provide the proper compensation for the past few years of becoming that new offensive threat. During the offseason, Butler was offered and signed for a five-year contract that is worth $95 million. This also allowed the Bulls to have an option on the final year of the contract. It was considered a maximum contract to keep him from leaving the Windy City. With the way he had played the last season and how the Bulls were intent on keeping him for a long-term deal, he had become the new face of Chicago that season.

There was a real chance for Butler to leave as he had met with other teams like Eastern Conference rivals the Boston Celtics and Philadelphia 76ers as well as Western Conference teams needing a star like the Los Angeles Lakers and Dallas Mavericks. However, the team's executive vice president John Paxson, a former player who knows greatness after having played with starters like Michael Jordan in Chicago, made it publicly known that the Bulls were going to match any offer that Butler received. Butler had the largest jump in points per game between the 2013-14 season and 2014-15 season at 6.9 points.

In addition to player news, there were multiple reports near the end of last season regarding the tensions that were building between head coach Tom Thibodeau and the front office staff of the Bulls. The team announced publicly to the media that a change was needed after five seasons. Even though Chicago was in the playoffs in each of those five seasons, none of those seasons featured the team advancing past the second round, and that included the previous season where they lost the Eastern Conference Semifinals in six games to Cleveland. The termination was made with Thibodeau having two years and about $9 million left on his contract.

Only a few days later, the Bulls announced the hiring of Fred Hoiberg, who had previously coached for the Iowa State Cyclones collegiate basketball program. There were not many surprises for NBA experts considering that it was not too much of a secret that the front office staff members at the Bulls' headquarters building were always interested in Hoiberg. He had even developed a friendship with Chicago's general manager, Gar Forman, over the past 20 years. You could credit part of that to being a former player in the NBA who had spent ten seasons with the Chicago Bulls.

During five seasons coaching for his alma mater at Iowa State, he accumulated a total record of 115-56 and made four trips to the NCAA National Championship Tournament, which included a 28-8 record and a trip to the Sweet 16 round in the 2013-14 season. He was not entering the league like many first-year head coaches who were with a struggling team that was well below the .500 record mark. Hoiberg had inherited a very talented team with a roster with a rising star, Butler.

It did not take long for Butler to show that he was worth the maximum contract in the Bulls' second game of the most recent season. On October 28, 2015, Butler made nine out of 11 from the field, which included making all three attempts from three-point range to lead Chicago with 24 points during their 115-100 win over the Brooklyn Nets. He also had six assists, four rebounds, and two steals. In the very next game, Butler was credited with his first double-double 23 points and 11 rebounds but made only 26.3 percent from the field and 12 of 14 on the foul line as the Bulls lost to the Detroit Pistons, 98-94.

While Butler had some good games, Chicago still had some struggles in the first half of the season due to recent signings and adjustments made by coach Hoiberg. A perfect example could be found on November 3, 2015, during 30-105 loss on the road to the Charlotte Hornets. Butler made 62.5 percent shooting (four of six from three-point range) to score 26 points. As far as the other starters in the game, Gasol had 13 points,

Mirotić had five, Rose scored four, and Tony Snell was shutout. In the next game on November 5, 2015, Butler was nearly perfect from three-point range (four out of five) to score 26 points again. The Bulls earned this victory over the Oklahoma City Thunder, 104-98. This time, Butler had support as Rose scored 29 points and Gasol had another double-double with 11 points and ten rebounds.

Butler scored plenty of games above the 20-point mark, and he hit a new career-high mark in scoring on December 9, 2015, in a 105-100 loss on the road to the Boston Celtics. Butler made 12 of 24 from the field and 12 of 14 from the foul line to finish with 36 points and seven rebounds. The support was not there to help the Bulls win as Gasol was the second-leading scorer with 16 points (while getting a double-double with 15 total rebounds), followed by Rose's 12 points, Doug McDermott's 11 points, and another ten from Mirotić.

As for another example of Butler having a great game in a losing effort, none could have been more frustrating than Chicago's 147-144 loss at home to the Detroit Pistons on December 18, 2015, in a game that took four overtime periods to find a winner. Butler led Chicago with 43 points after making 14 of 29 from the field (48.3 percent) and another 14 of 16 free throws while also collecting eight rebounds, two assists, two blocks, and two steals on defense. Rose also had a good game with 34 points and eight assists while Gasol had 30 points and 15 rebounds. Taj Gibson had 14 points and 12 rebounds, but the other seven players scored either single digits or none, including just three points from the fifth starter, Tony Snell. It was equally frustrating when Detroit had six players score in the double digits, and that included Andre Drummond leading the Pistons with 33 points and 21 rebounds.

Chicago was still maintaining a strong playoff position as this current season continued, and Butler continued to have strong games, even if he had a slow start. After scoring just two points in the first half, Butler finished with 42 points, five assists, four rebounds, and one steal during a 115-113 win in Toronto on January 3, 2016. Overall, Butler made 15 of 23 field goals (65.2 percent) and ten of 11 free throws. Butler was 14 of 19 in the fourth quarter alone. It was an impressive game for Butler, who broke the team record for most points in a half – a record held by the greatest Bull in Chicago basketball history, Michael Jordan, with 39 points in the second half of a 1989 game against the Milwaukee Bucks.

Only a few days later on January 5, 2016, Butler had another impressive game during a 117-106 win over the Milwaukee Bucks at home. After making 52.4 percent shooting from the field and a perfect eight for eight from the foul line, Butler had a total of 32 points while also having a first with ten assists in the win. It was also a solid game for the team overall as they shot 55.4 percent combined in field goals. Gasol had 26 points and 11 rebounds while Rose scored 16. All five starters were in double figures. This was the type of game that Chicago fans knew the team was capable of having. However, they were not able to be consistent like that every night. There was a three-game stretch later in January where Butler averaged 25 points but was still missing some shots. For example, Butler had 30 points, eight rebounds, and six assists on January 12, 2016, but he made just nine of 21 total field-goal attempts as the Bucks took the 106-101 win.

However, it was just a matter of until Butler had a game where he took numerous shots and had a high percentage made. During an overtime win, 115-111, over the Philadelphia 76ers on January 14, 2016, he went 15 of 30 from the field and 21 of 25 at the foul line to finish with 53 points as the primary offense for the Bulls. He also had ten rebounds, six assists, and three steals, and was the first Chicago Bulls player to score 50 or more points in a regular-season game since Jamal Crawford did it in 2004 during a 114-108 win over the Raptors. That was a

Chicago team that did not have the same success that the Bulls have had with the current regime of Rose, Butler, and Gasol.

Heading into the game with Philadelphia, Butler had an injured right ankle that kept him from participating in the pregame shootaround. It was the polar opposite of Rose, who was once considered the superstar for the Bulls franchise, who took part in the warm-up and then decided he needed more time to recover from some tendonitis. Even the writers who cover the Bulls daily admit that it is the type of storyline that is hard to make up.

Jimmy Butler eventually missed games because of that injury. Despite that, he was already selected by NBA coaches as a reserve for the Eastern All-Star team. That was the second time in his career that he was considered an All-Star. It was also proof that Butler was not merely a system player. Under Thibodeau, he made the All-Star squad for the first time in his career, but only after he got himself accumulated with the system for four seasons. However, under Hoiberg's entirely new scheme, he was still able to excel and make a name for himself as an All-Star. However, Jimmy Butler missed the midseason classic because of his injury. Replacing him on that team was Pau Gasol, his Chicago Bulls teammate that season.

Jimmy Butler made a successful return on March 5 just when the Bulls needed him the most. In that win over the Houston Rockets, he recorded 24 points, 11 rebounds, and six assists as if he were not gone for 11 games because of his knee injury. It just seemed like a typical day for Jimmy Butler, who had already shown defiance against his limitations and injuries. After that game, the soreness in his knee returned, and his back was also painful from compensating for his injury. He missed the next three games.

On March 14, Butler made a permanent return to the lineup in a win against the Toronto Raptors. He scored just 13 points while shooting a dismal 28% from the field. However, he got the win for his team and was showing signs of improved health. Three days later, he went for 22 points on an efficient seven out of 12 shooting from the floor to show how well he had progressed from his injuries. He also added seven assists in a win against the Brooklyn Nets that night.

The next time Jimmy Butler scored over 20 points was on March 31. In that win against the Houston Rockets, he tallied 21 points in addition to his eight rebounds and six assists. Butler shot eight out of 13 from the floor in a terrific one-on-one matchup with Houston's James Harden, whom he outplayed with his efficiency that night.

Two nights later, Jimmy Butler recorded his first career triple-double to solidify his claim as one of the top all-around wing players in the entire league. Against the Detroit Pistons, Butler put up 28 points on ten out of 25 shooting in addition to the 17 career-high rebounds he collected and 12 assists he dished out to his teammates. His defense was also excellent after he collected three steals and two blocks. However, the Bulls went on to lose that game. Butler made amends by winning the next game. He went for 25 points, five rebounds, and eight assists in that win against the Milwaukee Bucks a night later.

On April 11, Jimmy Butler had another terrific overall performance after tallying 23 points and 11 rebounds in only 29 minutes of play in a win against the New Orleans Pelicans. Two days later, he ended the regular season in what was his fastest triple-double performance to date. In a little over 25 minutes of play, he recorded ten points, 12 rebounds, and ten assists.

As the regular season wound down, Jimmy Butler led the team with 20.9 points, 5.3 rebounds, 4.8 assists, and 1.6 steals. He showed vast improvement in the way he created plays for his teammates even though Derrick Rose was healthy and playing that season. Butler then made the All-Defensive Second Team for a second consecutive season. However, his two-way play could save the Chicago Bulls from the disaster they were in that season. They failed to adjust to Fred Hoiberg's style and went in to barely miss the playoffs with a 42-40 record. They finished as the ninth seed after trailing two wins away from the Detroit Pistons for the final playoff spot. That was the first time in his career that Jimmy missed the postseason.

Final Year in Chicago

The Chicago Bulls team underwent a drastic change come the 2016-17 season. One of the first moves they made before that season was moving Derrick Rose out of his hometown of Chicago. The Bulls sent Rose to New York in exchange for Robin Lopez, Jose Calderon, and Jerian Grant. The trade officially ended the Derrick Rose era in Chicago while Jimmy Butler had fully become the team's leading man and franchise superstar.

The Chicago Bulls also actually acquired a new Chicago native. Dwyane Wade, who had spent his career since 2003 in Miami, had refused to renew his contract with the Heat. Instead, Wade had decided to return to his hometown of Chicago to have a chance to play in front of the people of the city he grew up in. Like Jimmy Butler, Dwyane Wade is also a product of Marquette. With Wade in the fold, Butler was moved to the starting small forward spot.

Other than Wade, the team also added point guards Rajon Rondo and Michael Carter-Williams. They drafted college standout Denzel Valentine and signed Paul Zipser, a former EuroLeague veteran. Losing Pau Gasol was a hard blow to the team, but they still managed to fill him in by putting Robin Lopez, who was acquired in the Rose trade, at the starting center spot.

With a combination of fresh talent teaming up with savvy veterans, the Chicago Bulls under Jimmy Butler's leadership were expected to make some noise in the Eastern Conference, especially considering that they had already acclimated themselves to Fred Hoiberg's system. Without Rose and Gasol, Butler was called upon to become the new leader of the team, though newcomer D-Wade had more experience and accomplishments under his belt.

Butler started the season going for 24 points and seven rebounds in the Bulls' opening day win over the Boston Celtics on October 27, 2016. With blowout wins against the Indiana Pacers and Brooklyn Nets, the Chicago Bulls seemed like a hungry team after starting the season 3-0. Butler did not even have to play 30 minutes in those two blowout wins.

Things started to normalize for the Chicago Bulls. By the time Jimmy Butler scored a then-season high of 39 points on a 13 out of 24 shooting clip on November 9 against the Atlanta Hawks in a loss, the Bulls had started the season 4-4 in their first eight games. Essentially, Chicago merely traded wins with losses as the season went by.

Despite a 4-4 start, Jimmy Butler later led a four-game winning run early in the season to give the Bulls a more ground in their wins. After getting the first of those four wins against Miami, Butler scored 37 points to go along with eight rebounds and nine assists in an 11-point win over the Washington Wizards on November 12. Three days later, he went for his first double-double of the season when he had 27 points and 12 rebounds in a blowout victory against the Portland Trailblazers. He finished the four-game run with a second double-double performance of 20 points and ten rebounds against the Utah Jazz. Butler averaged 26 points, nine rebounds, and 5.5 assists in those four games.

On November 20 against the LA Lakers, Butler went for a new season-high in a win. Going 14 out of 23 from the field and 12 out of 14 from the foul line, he scored 40 points while also collecting seven rebounds and dishing out six assists. Just two nights later in a loss to the Denver Nuggets, he went for 35 points on a 55% shooting clip.

Jimmy Butler had his third double-double of the season in a loss to the Washington Wizards on December 21. He finished that game with 20 points, 11 rebounds, and five assists. A week later, he had his best double-double game at that point in a win over the struggling Brooklyn Nets. Butler went for 40 points and ten rebounds in that match. He shot 14 of his 29 shots while making all 11 of his free throws that night. He thoroughly topped that performance just a few nights later.

Jimmy Butler opened what was to become a momentous 2017 by going for one of his best performances to date in a win against the Charlotte Hornets on January 2. Butler made 15 of his 24 shots and 21 of his 22 free throws in that game. He also finished the first half of that game with 20 points while scoring 17 clutch markers in the final four minutes. By the end of the night, Butler had arguably the best game of his career, though he was a point shy of his career-high in points. He finished with 52 points, 12 rebounds, six assists, and three steals in 38 minutes of play.

Five days later, Jimmy Butler had another similar performance. In an overtime win and a one-on-one showdown with the

Raptors' DeMar DeRozan, Butler went for 42 points, ten rebounds, and five assists to down Toronto and to outplay his counterpart over at the other end. Over ten days, Jimmy Butler had three games of scoring at least 40 points in a double-double effort. During that span, he averaged 34 points, 8.5 rebounds, 5.7 assists, and 2.3 steals in six games. Had those been his numbers the entire season, he had been a serious MVP candidate.

On January 20, Butler went for 40 points for a fifth time that season though it was in a loss to the Atlanta Hawks. Things were not easy for Jimmy Butler and the Chicago Bulls that season. After that loss to the Hawks, Butler was starting to question his role players' desire and effort to win games. The team fined him for those comments and held him out of the starting lineup in a loss to the Miami Heat on January 27. Incidentally, that was one of Butler's worst games that season. He shot one out of 13 from the field and finished with only three points.

All season long, the Chicago Bulls were having problems on the floor and inside the locker room. On the floor, it was chaotic. The new players could not mesh together in Hoiberg's system. Rajon Rondo's play was inconsistent, and he was a significant liability because of his lack of a consistent outside shot.

Dwyane Wade was getting old, though he was still putting up good numbers for his age. However, he did not shoot the ball well from the outside. The Bulls' lack of shooting only made it more difficult for a slasher and perimeter shooter such as Jimmy Butler to operate.

Things only got more chaotic in the middle of the season when Chicago traded away consistent veteran Taj Gibson and Doug McDermott, who was probably the team's best outside shooter. The atmosphere in Chicago that season was indeed troublesome and only got experienced players such as Butler and Wade frustrated because of how much they wanted to win.

What was even more surprising was that Chicago ownership and the Bulls' front office were not a hundred percent sure in making Jimmy Butler the face of the franchise and their cornerstone for the future. They were unsure of whether they would build around him even though Jimmy was putting up career numbers across the board that season. What they did not see in Butler or what they thought the star wingman lacked was a matter best explained by the team officials. At that moment, what was clear was that Jimmy Butler's days in Chicago were numbered.

Sometime before the trade deadline, the Bulls even put Jimmy Butler on the trading block and listened to potential deals involving the three-time All-Star wing. The most notable trade talk that happened was between the Bulls and Celtics. The Celtics were looking to bolster their East-leading roster by adding another star to ease up the scoring load on point guard Isaiah Thomas. Boston had several outstanding players that played their roles to perfection but lacked another go-to guy outside of Thomas. Butler had fit in perfectly with a passing team like Boston, especially since he never demanded the ball too much and played both ends of the floor at an elite level.

The Boston Celtics tried to offer a package that included some of the team's best role players but held out on dealing either Butler's Marquette teammate Jimmy Butler or perimeter defensive stud Avery Bradley. The Celtics' most enticing pieces were the 2017 and 2018 first-round draft picks they got from the Nets a few seasons back in the Garnett and Pierce trade. With how bad the Nets were playing that season, their pick fell somewhere within the top five. They were not expected to improve drastically in 2018, so their pick could still very well be a high lottery choice.

However, the trade never materialized. The Boston Celtics held out on trading one of their future first-round draft picks. Had they chosen to include those picks, any team in the league listened to them considering how deep the 2017 NBA Draft was looking to be. For the Chicago Bulls' part, they deemed Jimmy Butler untouchable at least for that season as they were still hoping for a playoff push. If they were to trade Butler, it would most likely happen during the 2017 offseason.

The trade deadline passed by, and Jimmy Butler was still with the Chicago Bulls. Despite all the rumors and the turmoil surrounding the team, Butler manned up and continued to lead the Bulls for a chance at a playoff position and at least go over the .500 mark in their win-loss record.

In one of his best performances after the trade deadline, Jimmy posted a double-double game on March 13 in a win against the Charlotte Hornets to show his unselfishness. He had 23 points and 11 assists while also grabbing six rebounds in that all-around performance. That win snapped a five-game losing streak for the Bulls, who were desperately trying to get back on the winning track.

On March 21, Butler's efforts were again in vain. He had a remarkable night when he went for 37 points, ten rebounds, and six assists. He even shot the ball well from everywhere on the court, whether it was on the perimeter or at the free-throw line.

However, the struggling Chicago Bulls lost that one to the Toronto Raptors even though their best player was putting up solid numbers.

Nevertheless, Butler made up for that loss with another unselfish night one game later. In a win against the Detroit Pistons, Jimmy shot only six shots from the field but made all of them. He scored 16 points. The stat of the night for Butler was his then-career-best 12 assists he dished out in that all-around effort. In his next game, he went for 36 points, seven rebounds, and 11 assists though the Bulls lost to the lowly Philadelphia 76ers. Wrapping up a four-game double-double streak, Jimmy Butler went for 20 points and a new career-high of 14 assists in a win over the Milwaukee Bucks. In those four games, he averaged 30 points, seven rebounds, and nearly 11 assists.

That win against the Bucks jump-started the Bulls' return to the winning track as they were fighting for the final few spots in the Eastern Conference's playoff picture. In the middle of all that was Jimmy Butler, who played excellent basketball in trying to lead his team to a postseason seeding. After that win in Milwaukee, he led the Bulls to three more consecutive wins.

The first win was against Cleveland, whom Butler scored 25 points on. After that, Jimmy helped beat the Atlanta Hawks by posting 33 points, five rebounds, and eight assists. Then in the team's fourth consecutive win, Butler went for 14 out of 26 from the field, three out of three from the three-point line, and eight out of ten from the foul stripe to score 39 points against the New Orleans Pelicans on April 2.

On April 6 when the Bulls were still 38-40, Jimmy Butler posted his fourth career triple-double and his second that season in a win against the Philadelphia 76ers. Pushing the Chicago Bulls to a 39-40 record, Butler had 19 points, ten rebounds, and ten assists in another spectacular all-around effort for one of the league's premier wing players. The Bulls tallied two more wins to finish the season winning seven of their final nine games. In those nine outings, Butler averaged 26 points, six rebounds, and 6.3 assists. He shot 52% from the floor to lead Chicago to a playoff seeding in those nine games.

By the end of the season, Jimmy Butler averaged 23.9 points, 6.2 rebounds, 5.5 assists, and 1.9 steals. Those were all career-highs for the three-time All-Star, who was getting better as he was still in the prime of his athletic form. He was also selected to the All-NBA Team for the first time in his career. According to the league's new collective bargaining agreement, an All-NBA Team selection qualifies the player for a supermax deal.

More importantly, the Chicago Bulls were 41-41 and were the eighth seed in the Eastern Conference. While critics had written the Bulls as early as their first four games in the first round considering they were about to face the top-seeded Boston Celtics, Jimmy Butler and his Bulls team tried their best to make the entire world think twice about doubting their capability to win.

In Game 1 against the Boston Celtics, Jimmy Butler helped pull off the upset of the first round by going for 30 points and nine rebounds in leading the Bulls to a four-point win. While others said it was merely a fluke, the Bulls took it a notch higher in Game 2 after winning it by 14 points. Butler had an impressive all-around effort of 22 points, eight rebounds, and eight assists in that outing. More importantly, the Bulls were 2-0 heading back home to Chicago to try and take Games 3 and 4 in front of their home crowd.

However, back in Chicago, the Bulls started to look like the troublesome version of themselves during the regular season while the Celtics got back to the form that made them the top seed in the East. The Bulls struggled in those two home games to drop the series to a tie at 2-2. Not even Butler's 33 points in Game 4 were enough to help his team win one game at home. As the series continued, the Bulls looked nothing like the team that won Games 1 and 2. They lost Games 5 and 6 by a combined margin of 33 points. Coming back to win the series, the Celtics finished the Bulls off in six games after starting 0-2.

That Game 6 loss to the Celtics marked the end of what was a rough and chaotic season for not only Jimmy Butler, but the entire Chicago Bulls organization as well. From what had transpired the whole 2016-17 season, it seemed like the Bulls were better off rebuilding and trying their hand at fresher and younger talent in the hopes of landing another future franchise star like Butler. It also appeared that Jimmy Butler had played his final game for the Chicago Bulls in that Game 6 loss.

In retrospect, it was indeed a tough season for Jimmy Butler. The Chicago Bulls signed players that clearly did not fit his game. D-Wade played shooting guard, which was Butler's playing position. Wade and Rondo were both ball-dominant players that took possessions away from Butler. From the looks of it, it was evident that Chicago did not want to build a team that fit Butler's playing style. Jimmy also did not fit well with Hoiberg's system while reports surfaced about tensions between them. All of those pointed towards Butler's eventual exit from the city and team he has played for since 2011.

The Trade to Minnesota, Leading the Wolves to the Playoffs

As expected, when the 2016-17 NBA season ended, and the offseason officially started, Jimmy Butler became the subject of trade talks again. It appeared that the Chicago Bulls were already intent on moving on from him to try to rebuild on fresher talent that could one day also improve to become the franchise star that the three-time All-Star was for them.

At first, there seemed to be only two top suitors that were looking to add Jimmy Butler to their team. The first one was Cleveland. The Cleveland Cavaliers were fresh off the NBA Finals where the Golden State Warriors dominated them in five games. Looking to match the Warriors' firepower of four All-Stars, the Cavs were intent on adding a fourth star to their roster to play alongside LeBron James, Kyrie Irving, and Kevin Love.

The problem with the Cavaliers' plans on trading for Jimmy Butler was that the Bulls were looking to get fresh young talent that they could build on for the future. The Cavs had none of that. They had no top first-round picks, nor did they have young talents that were looking to bloom elsewhere. Instead, what they had were veterans that they brought in to help win a title with LeBron. If the Cavs were looking to get Butler, they needed a third team to join the discussions. However, it never happened as Cleveland's plans of getting another star went up in smoke.

The second team that looked like they were in the running to become the next destination for Jimmy Butler were, of course, the Boston Celtics. Throughout the 2016-17 season, the Celtics were in constant talks with the Bulls in trying to acquire Jimmy Butler. However, no trade happened when the deadline passed due to the Celtics' reluctance of trading away either Crowder or Bradley. While the Celtics were now willing to part with either of those starters, the Bulls were more interested in the third overall pick that Boston possessed for the 2017 NBA Draft. With that third pick, the Bulls quickly jumpstarted their rebuilding process with a top-caliber talent from the draft. They quickly found a new franchise player.

However, the Boston Celtics found their draft pick too valuable to trade for Butler. With the cap space they had, they were able to sign an All-Star during the free agency period. In short, acquiring Jimmy Butler was not their priority. Their reluctance to part with the draft pick helped them. Had they traded it away, they lost their chance of landing a young talent from the draft while also losing a bulk of the cap space that they could use to lure in another star during free agency. Despite all the talks, Boston was not Butler's final destination.

When the discussions with the Cavaliers and Celtics blew up, another new suitor came into the trade picture. The Minnesota Timberwolves had all that the Chicago Bulls sought. They had fresh young talent and the seventh overall pick of the 2017 NBA Draft. It did not take long for a trade between the two teams to materialize.

On June 22, 2017, the trade that sent Jimmy Butler from the Chicago Bulls to the Minnesota Timberwolves became official. In exchange for Butler, the Wolves sent over high-flying young guard Zach LaVine and point guard Kris Dunn, who was the fifth overall pick of the 2016 NBA Draft but was yet to find his identity in the NBA. The Wolves also sent their seventh overall pick, which the Bulls used to draft seven-footer Lauri Markkanen, whom they were hoping would become the next Dirk Nowitzki. With that, Jimmy Butler was no longer a Bull and was on his way to Minnesota.

While Jimmy Butler's final year or two in Chicago did not work out the way he had hoped, he did leave a lasting legacy with the Bulls. Butler showed the team and the entire city of Chicago how far hard work could get a person. From being regarded as a role player at best coming into the 2011 NBA Draft, to becoming a defensive stopper and developing into one of the best two-way wings in the league, Butler showed improvement to his game every single season because of how hard he worked to make himself a better player.

Jimmy Butler's development into an All-Star also saved the Chicago Bulls, in a way. With the way Derrick Rose struggled every season to get back to his MVP form after multiple injuries, the Bulls had no draft picks or other scorers on the team to take over from where their former franchise star left off. Then came Jimmy Butler, who suddenly developed into a promising player the moment Rose went down with an injury. Butler eventually became the new face of the franchise after he became an All-Star and solid all-around player for Chicago in his fourth year in the NBA. Had he not developed into an All-Star, the Bulls had easily folded in the years following Rose's injury.

Butler also became one of the Bulls' best players after the Michael Jordan era. Derrick Rose was Chicago's first All-Star since Michael Jordan in 1998 made the team. Since then, Joakim Noah, Jimmy Butler, Luol Deng, and Pau Gasol have made that team. Among those four players, Butler holds the most appearances as a Bull with three. He is also arguably the franchise's second-best player during the post-Michael Jordan era. With his longevity with the team as well as his consistency in the six years he spent in Chicago, he might have arguably even developed to become a better franchise player than Rose was for the Bulls.

Putting his days in Chicago behind, Jimmy Butler said that he did not like how the Bulls handled his eventual trade. He was the face of the franchise, but the Chicago Bulls kept shopping him and making him feel like he was expendable. Some even said that communications between him and the front office were mishandled, especially when the Bulls were shopping him. This led Jimmy Butler to realize that he never wanted to be the face of a franchise. He wanted to be him, a player playing for whatever team.

While Butler had a chance to start fresh in Minnesota, he also had the opportunity to finally play with players that had as much talent as he had. He joined one of the youngest teams in the league. The Timberwolves boasted two untapped and developing talents in Karl-Anthony Towns and Andrew Wiggins. Towns had already solidified his claim as one of the best young big men in the league while Wiggins was still getting better year by year. They also had a collection of good role players that could make life easier for Jimmy Butler. Most importantly, being in Minnesota allowed Jimmy to reunite with Tom Thibodeau, who was his coach during his first four seasons in Chicago.

Still at the prime of his career at that point, Jimmy Butler was called to become the veteran leader of a young and scary Minnesota Timberwolves team that has not made the playoffs in more than a decade. The last time they made the postseason was when Kevin Garnett was still roaming in their paint as their franchise star.

While not necessarily the new face of the franchise, which is a term he liked to stay away from, Jimmy Butler is the only legitimate and proven star on the Wolves, though both Towns and Wiggins are up and coming future stars. As arguably the new leader of the team, Butler had plenty of work to do in mentoring his younger teammates but, in turn, the young talent that the Wolves have made it easier for him to strut his stuff out there on the court. With Jimmy in the fold, the Wolves were only going to get scarier as future playoff contenders.

Jimmy Butler needed to adjust with the Timberwolves first when he started playing with them in an actual NBA game. He made his Minnesota debut on October 18, 2017, in a loss to the San Antonio Spurs. In that game, Butler finished with 12 points. While he led the Wolves to wins in their next two games, he was more of an all-around player than a scorer. He had 13 points, seven rebounds, and five assists against the Jazz and then 15 points, six rebounds, and six assists in a win over the OKC Thunder.

In a win over the Oklahoma City Thunder on October 27, Jimmy Butler broke out of his slump and went for 25 points while making seven of his ten shots and 11 of his 13 free throws. He also added five rebounds and seven assists. Two games later, he went for 23 points and three assists in a win over the New Orleans Pelicans.

Jimmy Butler had his first double-double performance on November 13 in a win over the Utah Jazz. In that game, he finished with 21 points and ten assists as he was more of an all-around player than a scorer. He had a better all-around performance in a loss to the Detroit Pistons on November 19. In that game, Butler had 26 points, ten rebounds, four assists, and five steals. Then, on November 28, he had a similar performance when he went for 17 points, seven rebounds, and ten assists in a loss to the Washington Wizards.

As good an all-around player as he was for the Wolves, Jimmy Butler was a scorer first and foremost. In a win over the Los Angeles Clippers on December 3, he had a new season-high of 33 points in addition to the eight rebounds and four assists that he had. The very next day, he went for 30 points, five assists, and four steals in a loss to the Memphis Grizzlies.

It did not take long for Jimmy Butler to surpass his season-high. In a loss to the Philadelphia 76ers on December 12, the former Bulls franchise player went for 38 points on 15 out of 33 shooting from the field. Six days later, he went for 37 points, six rebounds, four assists, and two steals in a win over the Portland Trailblazers. Once again, he surpassed his season-high by going for 39 points on December 27 in an overtime win over the Denver Nuggets. In that game, Butler was a relentless attacker and went 16 out of 18 from the free-throw line. He also scored 12 of the Timberwolves' 14 overtime points.

After averaging only 17.5 points, 5.5 rebounds, and 4.5 assists from October to November, Jimmy Butler looked like the Chicago Bulls version of himself throughout December. In the 15 games that he played in that month, he averaged 26.5 points, 5.5 rebounds, 5.3 assists, and 1.9 steals. After failing to score 30 or more points from October to November, Butler exceeded that mark six times in a single month. Moreover, the Timberwolves ended up losing only five of those 15 games.

When 2018 began rolling, Jimmy Butler did not slow down. In his first game on January 1, 2018, he had 28 points while hitting all 11 of his free throws in a win over the Los Angeles Lakers. Two nights later, he went on to have 30 points while missing only two of his 18 free throws in a loss to the Brooklyn Nets. Then on January 10, he once again lived on the free-throw line by making 11 of his 12 free throws to score 26 points in addition to the seven rebounds, eight assists, four steals, and two blocks that he had in a win over the Oklahoma City Thunder.

Jimmy Butler had a good stretch of games before the All-Star Game after he was selected to take part in the midseason classic for the fourth consecutive time in his career. The run started when he had 30 points, eight rebounds, seven assists, and two steals in a win over the New Orleans Pelicans on February 3. After that, Butler had 35 points, five rebounds, and six assists in a loss to the Cleveland Cavaliers. He wrapped the run with 38 points, seven rebounds, five assists, and four steals in a loss to the Chicago Bulls in the first time he returned to his old city after getting traded to the Minnesota Timberwolves. During that three-game run, Butler averaged 34.3 points, 6.7 rebounds, six assists, and 2.7 steals.

During the All-Star break, Jimmy Butler made a decision to skip the All-Star Game because he wanted to focus on resting his body in preparation for the stretch run that the Minnesota

Timberwolves needed to perform well at to make it to the playoffs. The problem was that he ended up injuring his right knee in the very next game after the All-Star break. Jimmy Butler was ruled out indefinitely because of the injury as he needed to recover from the meniscus injury he underwent.

Because of his injury, Jimmy Butler was forced to miss 17 consecutive games during the stretch run for which he previously rested. During the time that he missed, the Minnesota Timberwolves lost nine games. It was clear that the Wolves needed him as they needed every win they could muster up to get to the playoffs. At that point, they were fighting for the final spot of the Western Conference.

Jimmy Butler's return on April 6 was very timely for the Minnesota Timberwolves. In that game against the Los Angeles Lakers, he finished with 18 points and four steals. Then, in a win over the Memphis Grizzlies three days later, he finished with 15 points. In the Wolves' final game of the season, they were in a playoff with the Denver Nuggets for the last playoff spot in the West. Wanting to lead the Wolves back to the NBA playoffs for the first time since the time of Kevin Garnett, Butler finished that win against the Nuggets with 31 points, five rebounds, and five assists.

At the end of the 2017-18 season, Jimmy Butler averaged 22.2 points, 5.3 rebounds, 4.9 assists, and two steals. He also shot a career-high 47.4% from the floor. More importantly, he made the Wolves a group of winners. For the first time since 2004, the Minnesota Timberwolves were able to make the playoffs. That was the time when Kevin Garnett was still at his prime.

Jimmy Butler needed only one season to lead the Timberwolves back into the playoffs. He was the leader that needed to put the winning culture into a team that lacked it. Moreover, he was the fire that made young players Karl-Anthony Towns, and Andrew Wiggins want to tap into their potential to become stars in their own right. As cold a region as Minnesota is, Butler was the fire the Wolves needed to make a return trip to the playoffs.

Unfortunately for Jimmy Butler and the Minnesota Timberwolves, they had to match up against the top-seeded Houston Rockets. On his part, Butler combined for only 24 points in Games 1 and 2, which were losses for the Wolves. His only great performance that series was on Game 3 when he had 28 points, seven rebounds, and five assists. However, the Houston Rockets eventually defeated them in five games after blowing them out in Games 4 and 5.

In the five games that Jimmy Butler played in the playoffs, he averaged only 15.8 points, six rebounds, and four assists while shooting only 44.4% from the floor. He and the Timberwolves were simply no match for the Houston Rockets in the playoffs. Nevertheless, if there was anything to take away from that season for Jimmy Butler, it was that he proved himself a leader. He had the competitive spirit and the skills to help lead an inexperienced and young team to the playoffs.

The Butler Saga, Moving to Philadelphia

During the offseason of 2018, Jimmy Butler made it known to the Minnesota Timberwolves that he had no plans of re-signing with the team when his contract expires during the offseason of 2019. Such was essentially a reason for the Timberwolves organization to trade Jimmy Butler for an asset or else they risk losing him to free agency for virtually nothing in 2019. The Wolves' owner wanted to trade him as early as possible.[xxiii]

However, the problem here was that head coach and team president Tom Thibodeau wanted to hold on to Jimmy Butler for as long as possible because he believed he could lead them back to another playoff appearance. He has always loved Butler's ability to play both ends of the floor well and thought that he was a great fit to his defense-oriented system.

There were times when the Timberwolves were close to making deals with the Miami Heat and the Houston Rockets. However, Thibodeau was firm in keeping his best player on the team even though that there was no assurance that he would be able to keep him in the roster past the 2018-19 season. As such, no trade during the offseason ever materialized, and Jimmy Butler was forced to play out his final year as a Timberwolf.[xxiv]

This all eventually led to a particularly interesting Timberwolves practice. In that session, Jimmy Butler teamed up with the Minnesota reserves against the team's best players. He was leading his team to a win over the Wolves' main squad. During that time, Butler was not short on talking trash to his teammates and the team's general manager saying that "they needed him" alongside other expletives. He was mostly targeting Karl-Anthony Towns and Andrew Wiggins, the Wolves' duo of young stars, and was saying that they could not win without him because they did not have the competitive spirit.[xxiv] Butler was dominating that practice session in every way as he not only went on to lead his team to a win but also make a point to the entire organization how valuable he was.

In an interview with ESPN, Jimmy Butler all but confirmed everything that had transpired in that practice. Saying that everything was all about his passion for basketball and that he could not contain his emotions, he admitted that it was not the right or proper way to get his message across. Nevertheless, Butler did say that it was all about him being honest because he believed that his teammates were afraid of being honest to one another.[xxv] After all, honestly saying what you think about the team is a big part of a winning culture.

Jimmy Butler did indeed return to the Minnesota Timberwolves lineup. The same interview with *ESPN* also revealed that he got a four-year $110 million contract offer from the Minnesota Timberwolves. However, Butler eventually rejected the offer not because he believed it was not enough for a star like him but because he wanted the Wolves to make it feel like they needed him.[xxv] It was never about the money for Butler, who has always put more emphasis on winning and feeling like he belonged.

Amidst the chaotic environment and the awkward set up between him and his teammates, Jimmy Butler suited up the following season even though there were reports that said that the Wolves had no plans of playing him while shopping him to other teams. Butler made his 2018-19 season debut on October 17, 2018. In that loss to the San Antonio Spurs, he finished with 23 points, seven rebounds, and four steals. Two nights later, he went for 33 points, seven rebounds, and four steals against the Cleveland Cavaliers in a win.

After averaging 21.3 points, 5.2 rebounds, 4.3 assists, and 2.4 steals in the ten games he played for the Minnesota Timberwolves that season, Jimmy Butler was finally traded. He was dealt to the Philadelphia 76ers, a rising contender in the East, for a package that included Robert Covington and Dario Saric. After two months of a problematic relationship with the Minnesota Timberwolves, the Jimmy Butler saga ended, and both teams got what they wanted. Butler was traded to a legitimate contender while the Wolves got some assets in exchange for the four-time All-Star.

Getting dealt to the Philadelphia 76ers was a good thing for Jimmy Butler. Not only were the Sixers young, but they were also talented. That young team could make it to the second round of the 2018 playoffs banking on the skills of their star duo of Joel Embiid and Ben Simmons. He was also going to be a good fit for the Sixers, who needed a wing defender and an all-around threat from the perimeter to complement Simmons' playmaking and Embiid's inside dominance. Butler teaming up with Embiid and Simmons meant that the 76ers were going to have a Big Three in an era where super teams rule the NBA.

Jimmy Butler made his Sixers debut on November 14 in a loss to the Orlando Magic. He finished that game with 14 points. Two nights after that, Butler found his groove with the team and hit 28 points in addition to the seven assists and two steals that he had in a win over the Utah Jazz. Then, on November 25, he went on to have 34 points, 12 rebounds, and four steals in a win over the Brooklyn Nets.

On December 5 and 7, Jimmy Butler had back-to-back explosive scoring performances. He had 38 points and ten rebounds in a loss to the Toronto Raptors. Then, a game later, he went for 38 points, six rebounds, six assists, and three steals against the Detroit Pistons in a win. However, such performances were a bit rare for Butler as a member of the 76ers because the team was stacked with players that could contribute offensively.

The final time that Jimmy Butler scored at least 30 points was on January 11, 2019. In that game, he finished with 30 points, five assists, and three steals in a loss to the Atlanta Hawks. Since then, he played within the flow of the offense not as a primary offensive player but as an all-around threat that could create shots, rebound, make plays, and defend at high levels. The Sixers were relying more on Joel Embiid and JJ Redick on offense while giving more opportunities to Simmons to make plays.

In that season, Jimmy Butler averaged 18.7 points, 5.3 rebounds, four assists, and 1.9 steals. He also shot 46.2% from the floor and 34.7% from the three-point line for the Philadelphia 76ers, who won 51 games and made it to the playoffs as the third seed in the Eastern Conference. He may not have had the same kind of impact that Embiid and Simmons had on the team during the regular season, but Butler's experience and ability to create shots for himself made him a critical asset during the playoffs.

Jimmy Butler opened the playoffs with 36 points and nine rebounds in a loss to the Brooklyn Nets in Game 1 of their first-round matchup. In Game 2, he ended up with only seven points but focused more on the other facets of the game to give his team a blowout win. Acting more as a defensive player throughout the entire series, Butler averaged only 12 points from Games 2 to 5 but helped the team win the series in five games after losing Game 1.

In the second round, Jimmy Butler found a crucial role as the primary defender on superstar wing Kawhi Leonard when the Sixers faced the Toronto Raptors. After posting only ten points in a loss in Game 1, Butler found himself going for 30 points, 11 rebounds, and five assists in Game 2 to lead his team to a win against the second seed in the Eastern Conference.

The Sixers were in for a tough series. The Raptors were a solid defensive team that had all the assets to stop Philadelphia's leading stars. They exploited Simmons' lack of a jump shot by sagging off him and focusing more on the other offensive players. This also allowed them to make things difficult inside for Joel Embiid, who struggled against Marc Gasol's defense and the Raptors' help defenders. As the Toronto Raptors were able to find ways to stop the likes of Embiid and Simmons, Jimmy Butler had to step up because he was the only player that could create his own shots off the dribble.

In a Game 3 win, Butler went for a fantastic all-around performance after finishing the game with 22 points, nine rebounds, and nine assists to put the Sixers up 2-1 in the series. He then went on to have 29 points and 11 rebounds in Game 4 as the Raptors went on to tie the series. In what was an embarrassing loss in Game 5, Butler had 22 points and seven rebounds in 30 minutes of action. However, he went on to lead the team in Game 6 after tying the series up to force Game 7. Butler finished that game with 25 points, six rebounds, eight assists, and two steals.

Game 7 was a particularly tough one for Jimmy Butler and the Philadelphia 76ers. In what was a defensive battle that saw both teams struggling from the floor, Butler had a poor shooting performance. However, he hit the most critical shot for the Sixers in that game when they were trailing to the Toronto Raptors by two points with only a few seconds left on the clock.

After completing a defensive stop, the Sixers' midseason acquisition Tobias Harris collected the rebound and gave the ball to an aggressive Jimmy Butler, who used all the energy he had to streak up the court while the defense was still trying to recover. Butler ended up hitting a tough layup over defensive big man Serge Ibaka to tie the series up 90 points apiece with 4.2 seconds left on the clock.

However, Jimmy Butler was unable to do anything in the final play of the game. In what seemed like a miraculous shot, Kawhi Leonard could hoist up a fading jumper at the right corner. The shot looked off at first, but after a few bounces, it made its way through the hoop as time expired. Butler's game-tying shot was put to waste as the Toronto Raptors won Game 7 in the most dramatic way possible. The Raptors eventually made it to the NBA Finals, where they defeated the Golden State Warriors to win their first-ever NBA championship.

Although Jimmy Butler failed to go deep into the playoffs with a stacked team that had stars and solid role players, it was still enough for him to retain his status as a legitimate star and as a player that could command a max contract. After all, he was arguably the Sixers' best player during the playoffs even though Philadelphia's leading stars were Embiid and Simmons. It was his experience and diverse set of offensive and defensive skills that allowed him to excel during the playoffs. The entire postseason, he averaged 19.4 points, 6.4 rebounds, and 5.2 assists. He excelled in the second round, where he averaged 24 points, 7.7 rebounds, and 5.7 assists in seven games.

As Jimmy Butler's season ended in the second round the same way it did back in 2015 and also in 2012, questions about his future with the team surfaced. He was going to be an unrestricted free agent in an offseason that was full of big-name free agents such as Kevin Durant, Kyrie Irving, Klay Thompson, and Kemba Walker. On top of that, he was undoubtedly deserving of a max contract. Were the Sixers willing to give him a lucrative deal at a time when they were going to be paying Embiid and Simmons large sums? It certainly was going to be difficult especially since they also needed to pay Tobias Harris and the other key players.

Signing with the Miami Heat

During the free agency period, Jimmy Butler did indeed leave the Philadelphia 76ers while also getting the max contract he deserved. Butler chose his destination for the first time in his career as he eventually decided to go to the Miami Heat. To make that deal happen and to give both parties the assets that they wanted, the Philadelphia 76ers dealt him to Miami in a sign-and-trade agreement that allowed Butler to go to the Heat while also acquiring capable two-way swingman Josh Richardson.

Now in control of his career, Jimmy Butler became the Heat's newest star and was probably on his way to becoming the new face of the franchise after Miami spent several years contending for a playoff spot without relying on a legitimate All-Star. This time, however, Jimmy Butler was not playing alongside fellow All-Stars and was going to be his own man in Miami.

It was shocking for him to want to go to Miami, especially when teams with All-Stars were interested in signing him during the 2019 offseason. He could have stayed with the Sixers to continue to play alongside a stacked and improving squad. He could have also chosen to go to the Rockets to team up with James Harden. The Clippers and Lakers were also viable options for him if he wanted to play for contenders immediately.

However, later on, Jimmy Butler revealed the reason why he chose to go to Miami even though that he was going to play for a team without All-Stars. It started when he toured Miami to try to get a feel of the place. Butler realized how the people of Miami loved basketball and how he felt like he was going to enjoy playing for that city and its people. Then the recently-retired Dwyane Wade, the former face of the franchise, pitched in and told Butler that he was going to be a good fit with the organization.[xxvi] That eventually convinced him to go to Miami.

Dwyane Wade was right. Jimmy Butler was an excellent fit for the Heat organization. Since Pat Riley took over the team during the 90s, the Heat were always about work ethic, great conditioning, and hard-nosed basketball. Regardless of whether they had stars or not, they were always a competitive team because of how they got players to buy into the culture and to chip in on the defensive end while playing hard on offense.

Jimmy Butler checked all off the boxes. Ever since he was drafted, Butler never stopped working hard to become a great player on both ends of the floor. He also fit the Heat's defensive mantra as he has always been a player that puts plenty of effort on that end of the floor. Moreover, his great conditioning and his competitive spirit were assets that the Miami Heat were looking for in their players.

The Heat organization has never had a stellar all-around player like Butler ever since LeBron James left in 2014. Now, they have one in Jimmy Butler. For the sake of both parties, the Butler era hopefully should work. After all, Butler needed a team to call his own, and the Miami Heat needed a new face to usher to lead the organization into the future.

Chapter 4: Butler's Personal Life

Long gone are the days where he had to find a friend who let him stay for a few weeks at a time during high school. Now Butler has his own home, and it was well worth the wait. Within a 40-acre property sits a mansion that has about nine bedrooms, 14 bathrooms, 30-foot vaulted ceilings, an infinity pool, and more than 13,000 square feet of living space that sits just outside of San Diego, California. He's not alone, as he resides there with two of his "brothers" from his childhood past, and when he is not training early in the morning during the offseason at a nearby high school, he is focusing on his skills and having his childhood friends join and help him on the workouts.

Another thing that might surprise people about Butler when he is not on the basketball court is that he has developed a friendship with Hollywood actor Mark Wahlberg, who has become a source of work ethic to keep trying to get better on his quest for the NBA Championship. The two met in Chicago when Wahlberg was filming the most recent Transformers film in 2013, and he made a stop at a training center in nearby Deerfield, Illinois hoping to find a basketball game. He found

Butler and asked him for a one-on-one match, which might have taken the Bulls star a little by surprise.

One night later, Butler was part of Wahlberg's group at a local bowling alley that gathered to watch one of the big boxing matches on television. Since then, they have texted often and arranged to meet up whenever possible, whether it is Butler visiting Wahlberg and his family during West Coast road trips during the NBA season or accompanying the actor on European vacations in the summer offseason. While seeing Wahlberg as a family man and husband, he saw the work ethic of one of the most popular stars of film and television training and going after the next milestone. For Wahlberg, it has been a great chance to see someone who is still in his 20s and who can control his destiny in basketball and life. The message Wahlberg told Butler is that "If you don't give it your all now, you're going to regret it." In many ways, Wahlberg had become the father figure that Butler never had, one who threw Butler a huge celebration party after he signed his $95 million contract to stay with Chicago when he was still a Bull.

Butler's full name reads as Jimmy Butler III. As it was discussed earlier, he never knew Jimmy Butler, Jr. growing up which, in turn, affects having much of a relationship with the first Jimmy Butler. The one whom sports fans know of did not have the greatest of childhoods after his mother kicked him out of the family when he was just 13. It is this Butler who still kept his birth name despite being disowned by the family attached to that name.

It is not something that Butler likes to think about too much. Butler is not a big fan of looking back on the past, which is why he removed his rearview mirror so that he could never look back. In a story in Chicago Magazine, Butler said he does not want the past to be the definition of him and that he would rather be known for the basketball career he is focused on having – hopefully with a couple of championship rings when it is all said and done. While life has moved on, he has re-established his connections with his family, and he keeps in contact with his father and mom, and they talk regularly.

Considering everything that has happened to Butler, it might explain why he has a ritual that he and his brothers follow daily: paying for the bill of the person behind you in the checkout line, regardless of if it is less than a dollar or a thousand dollar order. The focus is sharing the blessing that has been given to Butler and his family – both by blood and by friendship.

Chapter 5: Impact on Basketball

One of the most common things attached to the biggest names in basketball is when a player receives an endorsement deal from a top basketball shoe manufacturer. Now, Butler was formerly signed to an endorsement deal to be a spokesperson for the Adidas brand for the early years of his NBA career. In the 2014-15 season, Butler made a switch to the Air Jordan brand. The switch to another brand affiliation forced him to take a 75 percent pay cut in shoe endorsements. When one's current contract is worth about $16.4 million per year, it does not seem like a big deal. The reason Butler wanted to make the change was that he was having many foot problems that he said were linked to Adidas brand basketball sneakers.

During the time he wore the Adidas brand in the NBA, Butler had many toe injuries and multiple occurrences where he rolled one or both of his ankles. According to Butler, this was never an issue when he wore Jordan brand sneakers during his college days at Tyler Junior College and Marquette University. Another reason why Butler wanted to go back to Jordan sneakers was because of how he looked up to the Bulls legend while he was growing up in Tomball, Texas.

Since making the switch to Air Jordan, which is a brand that is owned by Nike but produced by the NBA legend, Butler has been seen wearing different types of Jordan sneakers. The most expensive shoes of the bunch are the Jordan Retro 20s that go for about $300 to the public. Right behind that is the XX8 SE basketball shoe that is about $250. Other shoes from Air Jordan that Butler wears include the XX9, Super Fly 3, Super Fly 4, Retro 6 and Retro 14 models – all of which are below the $200 price tag.

Therefore, being able to wear shoes with the name of his basketball hero makes the 75 percent pay cut seem extremely minute in the grand scheme of things.

"I do it because I love the game, for one," Butler said in a Chicago Sun-Times story in June of 2015, not long before he signed the maximum $95 million contract with the Chicago Bulls. "I think Mike takes care of his players. He's always saying how this is a Jordan family."

Family has been the one thing Butler has considered most critical when it comes to staying connected with his parents, his friends, or his teammates. Butler has continued to make a name of his own, similar to the legend he looked up to, Jordan, face of the Chicago Bulls franchise in the 1980s and 1990s. In that time,

Jordan won six NBA Championships (which came with six NBA Finals MVP awards), 14 NBA All-Star nominations, and a scoring title in ten different seasons. He finished with career totals of 32,292 points, 6,672 rebounds, and 5,633 assists. By the way, Jordan also has an NCAA National Championship from 1982 when he was playing collegiate basketball with the North Carolina Tar Heels.

Butler did not win a national championship when he was with the Marquette Golden Eagles. He has not won any scoring titles in the NBA, and he has not won a championship in his time in Chicago, Minnesota, and Philadelphia. Keep in mind, though, that Butler has continued to grow as an offensive threat and that Butler averaged a little more than 23 points per game in the 2015-16 season and nearly 24 a game the following year. While he has not won a title in the six years he has played in the league, it is well-noted that Jordan did not win a championship until his seventh year.

Jordan's scoring numbers are a lot higher than what Butler has reached so far. Jordan averaged a little more than 30 points per game in his 15 total seasons between the Chicago Bulls and the Washington Wizards. Butler played in a much different league in the 1990s than the NBA that has evolved over the past 20 years. One single player, no matter how good they are and how often people proclaim them as the "king" in the world of basketball, can ever win a championship – not just in basketball, but in any sport.

Butler does have the makings of being considered one of the greats. Yet, he was unable to win a title in Chicago as their lone franchise star. Even after leading a group of young stars in Minnesota and Philadelphia, he still was unable to reach the pinnacle of individual and team success. However, the future is still bright for Butler as he is still one of the most competitive all-around wingmen in the NBA.

As far as the impact that Butler has had on basketball, his story is a reminder that superstars do not necessarily have to come from high-profile backgrounds before entering the high-profile world of the NBA, the most elite of the world's professional basketball leagues. Sometimes, there might be a diamond in the rough that comes from a small town in Texas who does not get an offer to play Division I college basketball and has to settle for playing at a local junior college.

Maybe when he does get an offer to a program like Marquette, he has to sit on the bench and play only a few minutes here and there before eventually becoming a starter and leading his team to the NCAA National Championship tournament. Now that same player gets drafted with fans of the home team who are not happy at all with him being selected as he goes to the bench intending to prove himself again.

Now one of the top players in the league, Butler did not have to have quite the background that other NBA superstars had. Butler's work ethic and continued efforts to succeed were the things that built his name – one that is slowly but gradually becoming a legacy of its own not only in Chicago but for Minnesota and any of the other teams he might play for in the future.

Chapter 6: Butler's Legacy and Future

When looking at Butler's career numbers, he has averages of 15.6 points, 4.8 rebounds, 3.1 assists, 1.5 steals, and about half a block per game in six seasons in the NBA. In the past few seasons, Butler has consistently averaged more than 20 points per game and has even scored at least 23 points a night during his final two years in Chicago. Butler has also shown his defensive capabilities as he has amassed a large number of steals and blocks already in his career. While shooting about 45% from the floor and nearly 34% from the three-point area, he has also proven himself as an efficient wing scorer and shooter.

Every season, Butler is almost always one of the many high-profile basketball players who participate in a minicamp to help with the selection process for Team USA men's basketball in preparation for the Olympics and the FIBA World Championships. It is considered as one of the most significant signs of respect to be included in Team USA, and Butler has proven himself a valuable player for the squad after averaging more than five points a night during the Olympics in 2016.

After earning his recent maximum contract and with his numbers continuing to grow in the current season as of this writing, Butler is gaining more popularity, and it is also a bit refreshing to see someone who does not come from an athletic family with skills that are inherited from them. Nor is Butler someone who had millions of basketball fans talking because he skipped playing at the collegiate level like Jordan had before he came into the league and win six championships with the Chicago Bulls.

Butler spent much of his high school years growing up attempting to survive from couch to couch at friends' houses after his mother kicked him out of her home and he did not grow up with his father in his life. He did not receive offers to play at an NCAA Division I basketball program right after playing at a district-championship level at Tomball High School and had to settle for playing junior college down the road from his hometown at Tyler Junior College. Playing there eventually gave him the stage to show that he could play college basketball, and he joined a Big East Conference program – one of the toughest in the nation – with Marquette University.

While he was a first-round selection in the NBA after helping the Golden Eagles qualify for the NCAA National Championship tournament, he was second fiddle at first for an often-injured Derrick Rose. With those injuries came the opportunities for the next man up, and in support of Rose and

Luol Deng since his rookie season, Butler has developed himself into a superstar of his own. That is what makes him a lot more unique of a star in the NBA, more so than others who fall into that "superstar" category.

Now fans know whom Butler is, and his story is becoming more known to the casual fans who did not read about him in the Chicago newspapers and in the articles before the 2011 NBA Draft where he was the 30th pick. Fans are starting to see him as one who had to battle for his opportunities, both in terms of getting into college and professional basketball. It is a lot more respectable and admirable. In the end, none of it matters.

Butler does not care about how many points he scores in a game, nor how many times he pickpockets an opposing guard or forward for another steal. Nor will Butler care about how many votes he gets for the All-Star Game, if he makes the All-NBA's first team, or if he has a chance to win the league's Most Valuable Player award.

Butler is part of a mindset of wanting to win that NBA Championship. It is easy for a team to publicly say that they think they can win a championship this year. Butler said it best in a feature in the Chicago Tribune as someone who does not want to say just one thing when they want the actions to speak louder than any words spoken. "It's time to stop talking," Butler said. "We have to go out and make it happen." He also showed the same kind of competitive fire and spirit with the Minnesota Timberwolves in that infamous practice session.

The future is full of possibilities for Butler because basketball is a sport that is all about who has the best runs, whether it is referring to scoring a 12-0 run to overtake the lead in a game or having the 12-game winning streak to get home-court advantage in a playoff series. It is still a young career for Butler. He is still in the prime of his athletic career, and there could be a championship or two for him. There are numerous factors to consider, but if all things work out well for Butler in his new team, he could very well become one of the best players of this generation.

Rest assured, Butler will likely score more points to stay true to the "Jimmy Buckets" nickname given to him by his teammates.

Final Word/About the Author

I was born and raised in Norwalk, Connecticut. Growing up, I could often be found spending many nights watching basketball, soccer, and football matches with my father in the family living room. I love sports and everything that sports can embody. I believe that sports are one of most genuine forms of competition, heart, and determination. I write my works to learn more about influential athletes in the hopes that from my writing, you the reader can walk away inspired to put in an equal if not greater amount of hard work and perseverance to pursue your goals. If you enjoyed *Jimmy Butler: The Inspiring Story of One of Basketball's Best All-Around Shooting Guards,* please leave a review! Also, you can read more of my works on *Roger Federer, Novak Djokovic, Andrew Luck, Rob Gronkowski, Brett Favre, Calvin Johnson, Drew Brees, J.J. Watt, Colin Kaepernick, Aaron Rodgers, Peyton Manning, Tom Brady, Russell Wilson, Michael Jordan, LeBron James, Kyrie Irving, Klay Thompson, Stephen Curry, Kevin Durant, Russell Westbrook, Anthony Davis, Chris Paul, Blake Griffin, Kobe Bryant, Joakim Noah, Scottie Pippen, Carmelo Anthony, Kevin Love, Grant Hill, Tracy McGrady, Vince Carter, Patrick Ewing, Karl Malone, Tony Parker, Allen Iverson, Hakeem Olajuwon, Reggie Miller, Michael Carter-Williams, John Wall, James*

Harden, Tim Duncan, Steve Nash, Draymond Green, Kawhi Leonard, Dwyane Wade, Ray Allen, Pau Gasol, Dirk Nowitzki, Paul Pierce, Manu Ginobili, Pete Maravich, Larry Bird, Kyle Lowry, Jason Kidd, David Robinson, LaMarcus Aldridge, Derrick Rose, Paul George, Kevin Garnett, Chris Paul, Marc Gasol, Yao Ming, Al Horford, Amar'e Stoudemire, DeMar DeRozan, Isaiah Thomas, Kemba Walker and Chris Bosh in the Kindle Store. If you love basketball, check out my website at claytongeoffreys.com to join my exclusive list where I let you know about my latest books and give you lots of goodies.

Like what you read? Please leave a review!

I write because I love sharing the stories of influential athletes like Jimmy Butler with fantastic readers like you. My readers inspire me to write more so please do not hesitate to let me know what you thought by leaving a review! If you love books on life, basketball, or productivity, check out my website at claytongeoffreys.com to join my exclusive list where I let you know about my latest books. Aside from being the first to hear about my latest releases, you can also download a free copy of *33 Life Lessons: Success Principles, Career Advice & Habits of Successful People.* See you there!

Clayton

References

i.   Ford, Chad. "Jimmy Butler Finds a New Home, Hope." *ESPN.com*. ESPN. 18 June 2011. Web.

ii.   Eisenband, Jeffrey. "Jimmy Butler: From Homeless Texas Teen to NBA's Most Improved Player for Bulls." *The Post Game*. Sports Media Venures. 7 May 2015. Web.

iii.   "Jimmy Butler, Tyler J.C. Apaches, Small Forward." *247Sports*. N.p., n.d. Web.

iv.   "Jimmy Butler Bio." *Marquette Golden Eagles Official Athletic Site*. Marquette University, n.d. Web.

v.   "Jimmy Butler, Tyler J.C., Small Forward." *247Sports.com*. N.p., n.d. Web.

vi.   "Jimmy Butler." *Jimmy Butler NBA Stats*. Basketball-Reference, n.d. Web.

vii.   Powers, Scott. "Bulls' Derrick Rose Tears ACL." ESPN. ESPN Internet Ventures. 29 Apr. 2012. Web.

viii.   "Chicago Bulls Summer League Roster." *RealGM*. N.p., n.d. Web.

ix.   "Bulls Exercise Third-year Option on Butler." NBA.com. National Basketball Association. 30 Oct. 2012. Web.

x.   Isaacson, Melissa. "Source: Derrick Rose Cleared to Play." ESPN. ESPN Internet Ventures. 9 March 2013. Web.

xi.   Cowley, Joe. "Jimmy Butler sets franchise record, plays 60 minutes in Bulls' 3-OT win." *Sun-Times.com*. 15 Jan. 2014. Web.

xii.   Windhorst, Brian. "Jimmy Butler Staying in Chicago." *ESPN*. ESPN Internet Ventures. 1 July 2015. Web.

xiii.   Friedell, Nick. "Tom Thibodeau out in Chicago as Bulls Seek 'change in Approach.'" *ESPN*. ESPN Internet Ventures. 29 May 2015. Web.

xiv.   Friedell, Nick. "Fred Hoiberg Hired by Bulls, Confident in Transition from College to NBA." *ESPN*. ESPN Internet Ventures. 2 June 2015. Web.

xv.   Attfield, Paul. "Butler Tops Jordan's Bulls Record with 40 Points in Half." *NBA.com*. NBA. 3 Jan. 2016. Web.

xvi.   Bracy, Aaron. "Butler Scores Career-high 53 points to Lead Bulls over 76ers in OT. *NBA.com*. NBA. 14 Jan. 2016. Web.

xvii.   Cowley, Joe. "Jimmy Butler Will Try to Gut One Out…" *Chicago Sun-Times*. Sun Times Network. 14 Jan. 2016. Web.

xviii.   "Knicks' Anthony and Warriors' Green Hold Slim Leads for Starting Spots in Third Voting Returns." *NBA.com*. NBA. 14 Jan. 2016. Web.

xix. Johnson, K.C. "Jimmy Butler Calls It 'an Honor' to Play with Team USA in Minicamp." *Chicagotribune*.com. Chicago Tribune. 13 Aug. 2015. Web.

xx. Smith, Bryan. "It's Good to be Jimmy Butler." *Chicago Magazine.* Chicago Tribune Media Group. 19 Oct. 2015. Web.

xxi. Sheade, Blair. "Jimmy Butler Turns Down Adidas Endorsement Due to Feet Problems." *Chicago Sun-Times.* Sun Times Network. 25 June 2015. Web.

xxii. "Jimmy Butler." *Tackl.com.* N.p, n.d. Web.

xxiii. "Everything that led to Jimmy Butler getting traded to the Philadelphia 76ers". *SB Nation.* 13 July 2018. Web.

xxiv. Schwartz, Nick. "ESPN's Adrian Wojnarowski on why Jimmy Butler erupted". *For the Win.* 11 October 2018. Web.

xxv. Winfield, Kristian. "The 7 most savage moments from Jimmy Butler's interview with Rachel Nichols". *SB Nation.* 11 October 2018. Web.

xxvi. Helin, Kurt. " Why did Jimmy Butler choose Miami? It started playing dominoes in Little Havana". Yahoo Sports. 22 July 2019. Web.

Made in the USA
Columbia, SC
15 September 2020